Eco-efficiency: A Practical Path to Sustainable Development

A Reference for Eco-efficiency Partnership in North-East Asia

United Nations
E S C A P

ECONOMIC AND SOCIAL COMMISSION FOR ASIA AND THE PACIFIC

FOREWORD

During recent years, we have been receiving vivid news and scientific reports that are confirming the clear phenomenon of climate changes and its impacts. Simultaneously, we have witnessed increasing prices for fossil fuels which indicates that the security of global energy demand and supply is fragile; this has made people everywhere aware more of the interconnection between climate change and energy insecurity. The simultaneous occurrence of these two factors is making the political and business communities more perceptive about the socio-economic and environmental impacts of climate change and the need for more proactive action. Also, the cognitive changes have brought about ever-increasing investments in renewable or alternative energy. However, we are still lagging behind in terms of the actions required for effectively addressing both climate change and energy insecurity, while atmospheric changes increasingly cause dramatic impacts on the livelihoods of people around the globe.

In this context, North-East Asia faces even greater challenges than other areas of the world. North-East Asia as a whole has gained a more dominant position in shaping the course of the global economy and environment. The increasing share of North-East Asia in the global market for both renewable and non-renewable resources has been boosting the absolute demand for resources in the global market. In turn, the price of such resources is increasing and this holds great implications for economic development, particularly, in the developing world, as well as for global energy security. This condition also is enabling the subregion to attain critical power in shaping the face of the Earth, as the by-products of ever-increasing resource consumption end up as pollutants and greenhouse gases. Thus, the challenge is to identify a more environmentally responsible track for the current pattern of economic growth.

The imperative for this challenge is also confirmed by the <u>China Sustainable Development Strategy Report 2006</u>. It revealed a low level of performance for most North-East Asian countries. In the present report, the assessment of the Resource and Environmental Performance Index, which is based on the correlation between GDP and the consumption of major resources, i.e., fresh water, primary energy, steel, cement and common non-ferrous metals, ranks Japan, the Russian Federation, China, and the Republic of Korea on the Nineteenth, Forty-fourth, Fifty-fourth, and Fifty-fifth, respectively, among 59 countries. Although the assessment may not necessarily present the real picture of national performance in the context of sustainable development, it draws out an important lesson for most countries in North-East Asia: lesson is the imperative to explore a new path of economic development, which would foster the efficient and reduced consumption of natural resources, thus lowering the production of environmental externalities. In fact, the principle of such a path is found in the concept of the Resource-Saving Society of China and the concept of the Sound Material-Cycle Society of Japan, which are closely in line with Green Growth, a key approach of ESCAP for decoupling environmental impacts from economic growth.

In response to the subregional challenge, the Twelfth Senior Officials Meeting of the North East Asian Subregional Programme for Environment Cooperation (NEASPEC) held in Beijing, in March 2007, adopted the "Eco-efficiency Partnership in North-East Asia" in order to facilitate cooperation among NEASPEC countries in promoting sustainable development through a practical tool – the pursuit of eco-efficiency. The new initiative of NEASPEC on eco-efficiency is based particularly on the consideration of appropriate responses to the need for exploring green growth and for promoting synergies among existing national strategies. In addition, it is a subregional response to the Plan of Implementation of the World Summit on Sustainable Development, defining improvements in eco-efficiency as a key means for changing unsustainable patterns of consumption and production. That Plan particularly calls upon countries to increase their eco-efficiency by providing incentives for investment in eco-efficiency, and by collecting and disseminating relevant information.

The outcome of the previously mentioned Meeting is also the result of a series of discussions among NEASPEC member countries. The first serious opportunity for NEASPEC to discuss eco-efficiency was at the tenth Senior Officials Meeting in 2004, which discussed environmental pressures resulting from the current trend of economic growth in North-East Asia and reviewed the eco-efficiency concept as a policy tool for enhancing environmental sustainability. Subsequently, the Eleventh Senior Officials Meeting in 2005 and an expert group meeting in 2006 conducted an in-depth review of resource consumption and environmental impacts, relevant national policies and subregional joint actions. Based on the discussions, the present report has been prepared in order to present an overall picture of eco-efficiency and provide background information for future activities. As this publication illustrates, the application of the eco-efficiency concept to the level of national policy is relatively new. Thus, we still need to undertake in-depth conceptual and normative work in order to improve its relevance to macro-level actions. However, improvement cannot be realized solely through conceptual and normative desk work, but requires interactions among various stakeholders working in the real world. In this regard, I would be more than happy if this first, small attempt helps government officials, academics and members of civil society to share a common view on eco-efficiency and develop detailed and workable eco-efficiency measures.

Before concluding, I would like to extend my gratitude to the government officials and experts who shared their knowledge about eco-efficiency. They include Mr. Lu Wenbin, National Development and Reform Commission of China; Dr. Li Tienan and Dr. Liu Caifeng, China Standard Certification Center; Ms. Liao Xiaoyi, Global Village of Beijing; Prof. Chen Shaofeng, Institute of Policy and Management Science of China; Mr. Jang Yong Chol and Mr. Ri Cha Dol, Ministry of Land and Environment Protection of the Democratic People's Republic of Korea; Prof. Toshihide Arimura, Sophia University of Japan; Mr. Michikazu Kojima, Institute of Developing Economies of Japan; Prof. Masanobu Ishikawa, Kobe University; Dr. Aya Yoshida, National Institute for Environmental Studies of Japan; Mr. Baldan Enkhmandakh, Vice Minister; and Mr. S. Avirmed, Ministry of Nature and Environment of Mongolia; Dr. Kim Jae-youn, Korea National Cleaner Production Center of the Republic of Korea; Ms. Kim Hyeae, Green Korea United; Ms. Hahn Chai-Un, Korea Business Council for Sustainable Development; Dr. Lee Sang-heon, Korea Environment and Resources Corporation; Dr. Chu Jangmin, Korea Environment Institute; Dr. Yan Tsygankov, Russian Cleaner Production and Sustainable Development Centre, Mr. Alexander Pankin, Ministry of Foreign Affairs of the Russian Federation. In particular, I would also like to express my gratitude to Prof. Kim Jeong-In, Chung-Ang University, who as a consultant compiled information on eco-efficiency issues in North-East Asia and made a thorough analysis of those issues. Finally, I would like to express my thanks to the production team that made possible the publication of this report.

Rae Kwon Chung
Director,
Environment and Sustainable Development Division
ESCAP

ABBREVIATIONS AND ACRONYM

APERC	Asia Pacific Energy Research Centre
CDM	clean development mechanisms
CO_2	carbon dioxide
DESA	United Nations Department of Economic and Social Affairs
DJSGI	Dow Jones Sustainability Group Index
ECP	environmentally conscious products
EKC	environmental Kuznets curve
EPR	extended producer responsibility
ESCAP	United Nations Economic and Social Commission for Asia and the Pacific
ESI	Environmental Sustainability Index
EPI	Environmental Performance Index
FAO	Food and Agriculture Organization of the United Nations
GAV	gross added value
GDP	gross domestic product
GEF	Global Environment Facility
GHG	greenhouse gas emissions
GNP	gross national product
Ha	hectare
IEA	International Energy Agency
JPOI	Plan of Implementation of the World Summit on Sustainable Development (Johannesburg Plan of Implement)
Km3	cubic kilometres
KWh	kilowatt hour
MCED	Ministerial Conference on Environment and Development
MDG	Millennium Development Goal
MSW	municipal solid waste
Mtoe	million ton of oil equivalent
NEASPEC	North East Asian Subregional Programme for Environmental Cooperation
NO_x	nitrogen oxides
NSO	National Statistics Office of Mongolia
OECD	Organisation for Economic Cooperation and Development
PLSA	participatory living standards assessment
PPP	purchasing power parity
REEF	resource efficient and environment-friendly
REPI	Resource and Environmental Performance Index
SMS	sound material-cycle society
SO_2	sulphur dioxide

TFC	Total final consumption
TME	total material requirement
Toe	ton of oil equivalent
TOPS	tropospheric ozone precursors
TPES	total primary energy supply
tWh	terawatt hours
UNCED	United Nations Conference on Environment and Development
UNCTAD	United Nations Conference on Trade and Development
UNEP	United Nations Environment Programme
WBCSD	World Business Council for Sustainable Development
WSSD	World Summit on Sustainable Development
WTO	World Trade Organization
WWF	World Wide Fund for Nature
3R	reduce, re-use and recycle

Contents

Table

Figure

Box

EXECUTIVE SUMMARY

The challenges of sustainable growth in North-East Asia

Rapid economic growth and significant social progress have defined the economies of the North-East Asian subregion over the past two decades. Led by the impressive economic performance of China along with the steady economic leadership of Japan and the Republic of Korea, the subregion continues to show its dynamism in the midst of a volatile global economy. Associated with this remarkable economic growth however, are the environmental implications of the subregion's economic activities. With more than a decade of high growth rates, the subregion is also exerting tremendous pressures, perhaps the most intense among the regions in the world, on its ecosystems. As North-East Asia has limited natural endowments, coupled with high population concentration, rapid transition from rural to industrial economies and the growing shifts to highly urban lifestyles further intensification of the pressures on the environment threatens to undermine the sustainability of economic successes for which the countries in the subregion are associated with.

North-East Asian economies face the serious challenge of sustaining the economic and social progress it has achieved without overdrawing its natural capital beyond their restorative capacity or does not become sinks for the residuals produced. But majority of North-East Asian countries continue to pursue growth patterns that are still inefficient, and resource and pollution intensive. North-East Asian economies rely heavily on natural resources and the environment to fuel their growth and as the subregion is resource-constrained it greatly pays on the price of resource commodities purchased in the international market. Fueling the demand for more resources is North-East Asia's industrial base which is oriented towards the export markets. Because the subregion has become the "global production centre" for export goods, the production processes also leaves behind many undesirable by-products including pollution damages and associated health costs adding burden to an already stretched capacities for managing the environment.

The importance of setting up a collaborative environmental initiative in North-East Asia has long been recognized that in 1993, under the auspices of the United Nations Economic and Social Commission for Asia and the Pacific (ESCAP), the North East Asian Subregional Programme for Environmental Cooperation or NEASPEC was launched. The cooperation programme was directed towards promoting environmental and sustainable development cooperative efforts for enhancing the quality of life and well-being of the peoples of the participating countries. Since its establishment, the cooperation embarked on a number of subregional and national initiatives aimed at strengthening capacities of institutions engaged in the promotion and implementation of sustainable development interventions. Early activities of the programme focused on the general aspects of environmental management specifically on pollution control and management and nature conservation and protection.

But new realities in North-East Asia necessitate a review of the current NEASPEC activities. Existing NEASPEC programmes, while remaining highly relevant, are also considered inadequate in responding to emerging environment and sustainable development issues. The challenge of easing the pressure on the environment brought about by the steady and rapid economic growth rates of North-East Asian countries demand a new development paradigm that advocates for green growth as a new thrust of cooperation in the region. At the core of this new thrust is in understanding the concept of eco-efficiency as a clear option for responding to the emerging challenges of sustainable development in North-East Asia. Underpinning this new direction is the imperative for strengthening NEASPEC to adopt and actively promote the eco-efficiency concept as part of the growth strategy of North-East Asian economies.

Imperatives for promoting eco-efficiency
in North-East Asia

The imperatives for North-East Asian economies to pursue a sustainable pattern of economic growth have never been more pressing than now. The subregion's ecological footprint and biological capacity (or biocapacity) provides a glimpse of the sustainability of current economic activity and trends for the future. North-East Asia's ecological footprint, a measure of environmental pressure arising from the consumption of a specified population, is calculated at **2.8 global hectares per person**, 30 per cent above the global average. On the other hand, its biocapacity, which is a measure of the total biological production capacity per year of a given area, is **1.9 global hectares per person** (excluding Mongolia since given its low population density contributes to a large biocapacity). The resulting ecological deficit is **0.9 global hectares per person**: implying that the present demands on North-East Asia's natural capital is being spent faster than its rate of regeneration. The scenario for North-East Asian countries is unmistakable: unless economic growth is decoupled from environmental resource use, their ecological footprint will continue to increase while their carrying capacity steadily decreases. The future implications for North-East Asian economies can be dire as current patterns can undermine the very base of their economic growth. Obviously hindering growth and lowering the quality of life are unacceptable outcomes but much more so is a collapse of the environment and ecosystems. A justifiable alternative for averting this unsustainable pattern of growth is for North-East Asian economies to improve their ecological efficiency (or eco-efficiency).

Noting the diverse economies of North-East Asia, developing countries of the subregion raises a fundamental question as to which model(s) of development is suitable for them. Even the two developed economies of the subregion, Japan (GDP/capita at PPP (2004) US$29,900) and the Republic of Korea (GDP/capita at PPP (2004) US$21,305), exhibits different patterns of growth. Japan in its early stages of industrial development has extensively used natural resources, importing almost all of raw materials to fuel its growth, but it has made a dramatic shift in their production and consumption patterns in the 1970's to become more resource efficient. The Republic of Korea, on the other hand, has patterned its growth with United States of America model which production and consumption patterns are not necessarily resource efficient. This pattern is manifested by looking at the footprint change per person of countries wherein the Republic of Korea has shown even higher footprint changes per person at 148 per cent than United States (38 per cent) and Japan (30 per cent) for the period 1975-2003. In the same manner, the Republic of Korea's biocapacity change per person (-35 per cent) is also higher than United States (-20 per cent) and Japan (-16 per cent). It would be interesting to note which pattern of growth will China, the Democratic People's Republic of Korea, the Russian Federation and Mongolia will pursue as they aspire to also rapidly develop in the future.

This publication advocates for a new paradigm for economic growth. The current planning approach for economic growth emphasizes only on economic efficiency based on market price. Unfortunately, market prices do not reflect the ecological price and thus, results to the abuse of the resources and ecological inefficiency of the economic system. A clear illustration of this inefficiency is the cost of traffic congestion in urban areas. Traffic congestion due to insufficient investments for public transportations such as railways, subways and an efficient bus system is becoming a serious problem in rapidly urbanizing countries in the subregion. The high congestion cost in the Republic of Korea and China due to their concentration of investments in highways instead of the mass transport system is costing them 3-4 per cent of their GDP. The prevailing development paradigm presupposes the attainment of economic efficiency, which is to bolster the growth of GDP, takes precedence over the agenda of protecting the environment. This outlook however, is increasingly being recognized as flawed for two reasons: First, the cost of the natural resources and environment in the present models of growth is usually undervalued and are not captured in the accounting of the national income; second, the market price is usually less than the environmental cost which is theoretically the sum of resource depletion and impacts of pollution. Concentrating on economic efficiency is antecedent for further abuse and misuse of ecological resources. The real issue is how one closes the gap between the economic efficiency and ecological efficiency. And internalizing the environmental costs is the most practical avenue for improving ecological efficiency of the economic system.

The adoption of the eco-efficiency philosophy is a sound approach for pursuing sustainable development since it argues for the continued promotion of economic growth and addressing the unmet basic needs of people without compromising the limited ecological carrying capacity of countries. Chapter 4 of Agenda 21 which dealt with changing consumption (and production) patterns planted the seed for promoting eco-efficiency. The Plan of Implementation of the World Summit on Sustainable Development [Johannesburg Plan of Implementation] (JPOI) was more explicit in its call for "increase(d) investment for cleaner production and eco-efficiency in all countries through *inter alia,* incentives and support schemes and policies directed at establishing appropriate regulatory, financial and legal framework". At the Fifth Ministerial Conference on Environment and Development in Asia and the Pacific held in March 2005 in Seoul, Republic of Korea, ministers from the 52 countries comprising the Asia and Pacific region endorsed the Seoul Initiative on Environmentally Sustainable Economic Growth (Green Growth) wherein one of its key targets is the improvement of eco-efficiency for environmental sustainability. After more than a decade of assessing the actual state of the global environment, greater confidence have already been built based on available knowledge and information and learned experiences on eco-efficiency which should impel societies to recognize that a much more desirable option for sustainable development is available.

How can eco-efficiency be achieved? The critical importance of shifting to a more efficient production and consumption patterns

Eco-efficient societies require dramatic shift in their current patterns of production and consumption. The idea of eco-efficiency stemmed from the evolving discussions of the environmental Kuznets curve (EKC) which hypothesized the relationship between environmental degradation and income per capita. Earlier discussions of the EKC theory argued that in the initial stages of economic growth environmental degradation and pollution correspondingly rises, but peaking at a certain income per capita level when the trend starts to reverse, so that further rise in income growth leads to an environmental improvement. Many development practitioners believe that the EKC has become the backbone of the current growth model of "growing up first and cleaning up later". Over the years the theory has been the subject of review and empirical studies testing the validity of the relationship, applying varying methodologies in different types of economies. The review results were found to be mixed wherein some economies found that the EKC exists but do not necessary hold true for many of the environmental impacts. At the crux of the eco-efficiency discussions is in understanding the current patterns of production and consumption of societies and defining the policy framework and parameters for which these patterns can be made more efficient.

The pursuit of eco-efficiency should be made in improving efficiencies in both production and consumption patterns. With the anticipated rise in incomes, production patterns of countries are also expected to improve with economic structures shifting to higher dependence on service-based and knowledge-intensive activities, and increasingly import, rather than produce, resource and pollution-intensive goods. But that is only one side of the formula. Improvements in income per capita can also spur conspicuous and discretionary consumption that could intensify the environmental pressures on the environment. Such trend can undermine the efficiency gains at the production side. The rapid expansion of urban centres in the subregion is already manifesting this pattern. Policymakers need to pay attention to these nuances as these issues can become entrenched in the growth patterns of the countries making the shift to eco-efficiency difficult to achieve.

Eco-efficiency efforts on the production side are notably led by the private sector, in particular the major industrial players. Industry leadership is understandable given the imperatives for which they have to improve their efficiency in resource and material use. In general, the adoption of eco-efficiency principles in the production patterns can be immediate inasmuch as the drivers for shifts can be mandated by policies and/or are market response to a particular stimuli i.e. cost-effectiveness of compliance, technology improvements and responses to consumer behaviour or demand. Moreover, the strategic environmental value of adopting eco-efficiency in the production process can strengthen the market position of the companies thus fortifying their competitive edge over other players that have not adopted the process.

Although eco-efficiency for production is steps in the right direction, these efforts however, are not sufficient in ensuring overall eco-efficiency. Equal attention would also have to be made to ensure eco-efficiency of the consumption patterns. But promoting eco-efficiency in the consumption patterns present more complex challenges than the initiatives for improving efficiency for production. The approaches will need to understand the factors that push consumers to behave in a particular pattern. Targeting policies and specific programme of actions that stresses voluntary actions through education and market incentives are important but it would need macro-level consumption policies that would ensure eco-efficiency is comprehensively pursued. Macro-level polices can cover as much ground with the objective of influencing consumer behaviour in the choice of their actions. For example, infrastructure policies that underscore eco-efficiency can promote investments for efficient transportation systems. Instead of constructing more roads and highways which induces consumer to use individualized vehicles, investments can be made on interconnected mass public transport systems which can bring more people to particular destinations. This initiative can also be complemented by market based regulations such as the levying of higher taxes for larger cars, imposition of road-users tax or congestion charges.

Eco-efficiency initiatives in North-East Asia

North-East Asian countries recognize their needs for a comprehensive and holistic approach to build eco-efficient economies. They acknowledge the necessity to fundamentally shift their current economic patterns of growth, implying to also change the way their consumers and producers behave. Within the subregion two countries have made initiatives to move towards eco-efficient economies: China through their Resource Efficient and Environment-Friendly (REEF) Society and Japan's 3R Initiative.

China's REEF is directed towards "conserving resources, improving utilization efficiency, sustainable economic growth with fewer resources in the process of production, construction, circulation, consumption, etc. by taking measures such as structural adjustment, technology improvement, enhanced management, further reform, promotion, etc." It is a reflection of the growing concern of China that unless a shift is made from their current patterns of growth, their economy may overheat which could threaten the long-term sustainability of their economic development. The 'REEF Society' strategy breaks down into two aspects: a wide range of integrated means will be applied to rationally relocate, recycle and reuse resources in a highly efficient manner at every point of production and consumption; and pollutant generation and other environmental impacts of production and consumption will be minimized. This resource saving strategy became a basic national development policy in 2005 and was incorporated in their comprehensive Five-Year-Plan.

For Japan the Waste Management Law laid a foundation for further endeavors in 'pollution diet' and environmentally sound management of waste. The nation-wide '3R Initiative' (reduction of waste, increase reuse and recycling of resources) for a sound material cycle-society was officially launched by Japanese Prime Minister and adopted by G8 Meeting in 2004 as part of G8 Action Plan. The 3Rs serve as the guiding principles of production and consumption for the government, corporate and civil society to achieve the scenario switch of material consumption. The centerpiece of the initiative is that instead of being seen as things to be disposed of, waste is regarded as valuable resources for further use. The 3R Initiative is believed to bring multi-folded benefits to the society: harmonizing environmental and economic concerns at the national level, minimizing waste at local level, serving as a driving force for increasing resource productivity and thus, competitiveness of industries, and facilitating citizens' hands-on contribution to a better environment.

Pushing forward the eco-efficiency initiatives in North-East Asia

Central to pushing eco-efficiency initiatives in the region is the need to close the gap between the economic price and ecological price. The Chairman of the Worldwatch Institute and former Vice President of ESSO Norway, Mr. Oystein Dahle captured in essence the value of closing the gap between the economic price and ecological price when he cited that "socialism collapsed because it did not allow prices to tell the economic truth. Capitalism may collapse because it does not allow prices to tell the ecological truth." There are a plethora of options for which these can be achieved namely; through the application of market-based instruments, regulatory instruments, voluntary measures, and information-based measures. In the past, all governments have focused on the application of regulatory instruments, such as command-and-control legislation that prohibits the use of certain technologies or mandates the use of others. This modality is not sufficient enough to correct the continued degradation of the environment in spite of the impressive rise in per capita incomes. Clearly, lessons from these experiences illustrate that the economic price of growth do not reflect the cost of the ecological damages arising from the economic activities. Until recently, governments are beginning to shift towards a mixed slate of policy choices, with a number of market-based incentives. The key to harnessing eco-efficiency is to use a wide range of policy tools that affects a large scope of society and inspire behavioral changes.

It has been stressed in this paper that moving towards eco-efficient consumption is probably the most important, yet most difficult, task ahead for North-East Asia. This paper intends to offer suggestions for achieving an ecologically efficient pattern of growth. The gist of proposed actions covers the following:

- Government Actions - At the macro-economy-wide level, North-East Asian countries should build and support a societal consensus on the objective of sustainable. development in an eco-efficiency framework. Governments need to reform their public policies in order to promote eco-efficient production and consumption at all levels, including government activities, consumer and producer activities, and international policies and regulations.

- Business Sector Actions - Private corporations have always been the starting point for eco-efficiency initiatives. Undoubtedly, without their participation and leadership, society will not be able to achieve its eco-efficiency goals. To that end, the private sector is expected to continuously work in integrating the eco-efficiency philosophy in their business strategies and production processes. However, it is important to bear in mind that the private sector alone cannot achieve eco-efficiency for society and governments need to support actions of the private sector through a reward or merit system that recognizes the positive eco-efficiency impacts.

- Civil Society Actions - Civil society's cooperation and positive response to eco-efficiency strategies promoted by governments and the private sector are extremely crucial in the entire eco-efficiency initiative. Central to their role is the acceptance of community responsibility vis-à-vis to their consumer rights and their understanding and support for demand-side management.

Role of NEASPEC

Regional efforts towards eco-efficiency should build a common vision for an eco-efficient society. NEASPEC, as an intergovernmental mechanism, can help establish this common vision and raise awareness by working with member countries in facilitating discussions for improving resource efficiency and disseminating information on eco-efficient practices across various sectors. It can start by undertaking comparative assessment of how countries in the North-East Asian region are faring in their efforts to attain eco-efficiency, distilling lessons from both the successes and failure of the efforts for which countries can learn and base their future eco-efficiency strategies. Similarly it can stimulate the promotion of eco-efficiency initiatives through capacity development, such as training programmes about eco-efficient practices across sectors and levels of society that will help strengthen the national, as well as regional, efforts for achieving eco-efficient societies. Additionally, NEASPEC can support and encourage information sharing and policy consultations, thereby assisting countries in institutionalizing policy frameworks for eco-efficiency. Steps in this direction have already been taken following the decision of the Twelfth Senior Officials Meeting in March 2007 to launch the Eco-Efficiency Partnership in North-East Asia. On this basis, NEASPEC will now develop a platform for joint activities for the promotion of eco-efficiency in the subregion. By employing multilateral actions mentioned above, NEASPEC will contribute to a sound foundation for an eco-efficient future for NEASPEC countries.

1. PROMOTING ECO-EFFICIENCY IN NORTH-EAST ASIA

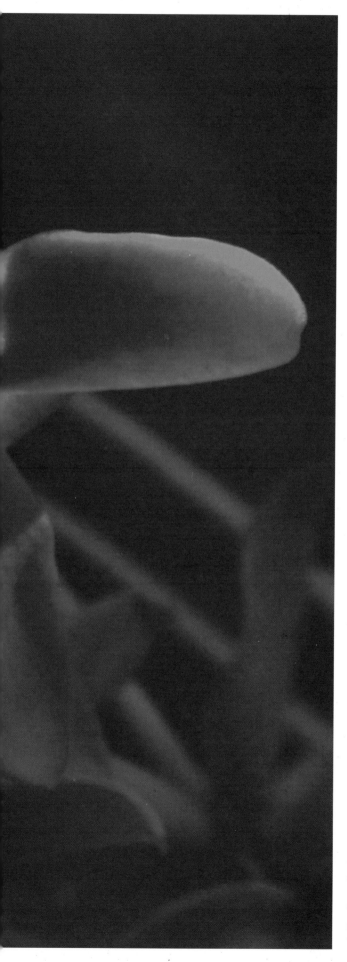

1.1 Overview

Societies' understanding of sustainable development continues to evolve since the development paradigm was embraced at the historic 1992 Rio Earth Summit. The world has accomplished significant progress in pursuit of the goals of Agenda 21, the blueprint of sustainable development, with more laudable efforts being carried out to maintain this momentum. Economic growth remains the engine for social progress and environmental changes. For more than three decades, the developing countries of Asia-Pacific have shown remarkable growth rates that allowed them to redress pressing social issues such as reducing poverty, limiting child mortality and providing basic services. This steady growth over the years has even made many developing countries resilient to withstand any political, financial and natural crises. Undoubtedly the agenda of rapid economic growth will continue to define future prospects for most of the developing countries in the region.

While this positive economic outlook is welcomed, governments also recognize other factors that could have significant implications in sustaining the current growth patterns. The Asia and the Pacific region has two thirds of the global population majority of which are poor, malnourished and lacks basic services; a situation that clearly underscores why sustaining growth is imperative. On the other hand, the region has limited natural resource endowments. It has the lowest freshwater availability per capita compared with other regions of the world, a biologically productive area per capita that is less than 60 per cent of the global average, and an arable and permanent cropland that is less than 80 per cent of the global average (ESCAP, 2005).

Albeit, in spite of the positive growth and development attained, the challenges of achieving sustainable societies have remained complex and difficult. The current state of every known ecosystem in the region establishes the undeniable fact that the environmental problems have become worse rather than better – an indication that existing efforts remains inadequate in reversing the unsustainable patterns of development. The challenge of development in Asia and the Pacific is clear: pursuing a development path that ensures economic growth and social progress while the natural capital are not overdrawn beyond their restorative capacity or does not become the sinks of residuals produced in the course of the development. Unfortunately, most developing countries continue to pursue growth patterns that are, in the context of new realities, as wasteful, inefficient and inequitable. With the natural capital serving as a limiting factor for development, the urgency to shift away from the conventional mode of economic growth pattern and move towards the promotion of eco-efficiency has never been more vital in the Asia-Pacific region.

1.2 The North East Asian Subregional Programme for Environmental Cooperation (NEASPEC): pursuing environmental sustainability in North-East Asia

North-East Asia economies present an interesting case for examining the approach to implementing the sustainable development goals. Making up over 44 per cent of the entire population of Asia and the Pacific, the countries of North-East Asia, which cover China, Democratic People's Republic of Korea, Japan, Mongolia, Republic of Korea and the Russian Federation varies in size and diversity in their economies. They vary in size from the world's largest, the Russian Federation to the relatively modest Republic of Korea. Their economies range from the second largest in terms of GDP (Japan) to one of the smaller economies in the world (Mongolia). This diversity creates vast potential for extensive subregional cooperation as the North-East Asian countries can complement and supplement their efforts according to the strength and weaknesses of their respective economies.

The importance of setting up a collaborative environmental initiative in North-East Asia has long been recognized that in 1993, under the auspices of the United Nations Economic and Social Commission for Asia and the Pacific (ESCAP), the North East Asian Subregional Programme for Environmental Cooperation or NEASPEC was launched. The cooperation programme was directed towards promoting environmental and sustainable development cooperative efforts for enhancing the quality of life and well-being of the peoples of the participating countries. Since its establishment, the cooperation embarked on a number of subregional and national initiatives aimed at strengthening capacities of institutions engaged in the promotion and implementation of sustainable development interventions. Early activities of the programme focused on the general aspects of environmental management specifically on pollution control and management and nature conservation and protection.

"The challenge of easing the pressure on the environment brought about by the steady and rapid economic growth rates of North-East Asian countries demand a new development paradigm that advocates for green growth as a new thrust of cooperation in the region".

But new realities in North-East Asia necessitate a review of the current NEASPEC activities. Existing NEASPEC programmes, while remaining highly relevant, are also considered inadequate in responding to emerging environment and sustainable development issues. The challenge of easing the pressure on the environment brought about by the steady and rapid economic growth rates of North-East Asian countries demand a new development paradigm that advocates for green growth as a new thrust of cooperation in the region. At the core of this new thrust is in understanding the concept of eco-efficiency as a clear option for responding to the emerging challenges of sustainable development in North-East Asia. Underpinning this new direction is the imperative for strengthening NEASPEC it to adopt and actively promote the eco-efficiency concept as part of the growth strategy of North-East Asian economies.

1.3 Why eco-efficiency?

The touted economic success and social progress achieved by the countries of North-East Asia have also brought daunting environmental issues. The push for rapid economic growth, high and rising incomes, urbanization, and changing lifestyles has been symptomatic of the environmental sustainability and increasing pressure on the natural environment. The 2005 State of the Environment Report for Asia and the Pacific highlighted the gravity of the environmental issues confronting the North-East Asia; growth based on rapid industrialization and rising incomes has lead to increasing pollution (air and water) and generation of waste and residuals (solid waste and e-waste); coastal and marine environment are rapidly deteriorating due to pollution and excessive exploitation of resources; deforestation and land degradation are creating serious subregional environmental challenges.

The drive for sustaining growth in the face of rising environmental pressures and a deteriorating natural resource base are sufficient grounds to search for better options for development in the North-East Asian subregion. The considerations are clear: hindering growth and lowering standards of living are unacceptable choices but much more so is a collapse of the environment and ecosystems. Several models of development are available but the fundamental question of governments is which of these models warrant a continuing process of economic growth without unnecessarily overshooting the available but limited natural capital.

This makes eco-efficiency a justifiable and viable alternative to the current development patterns. The theoretical fundamentals of eco-efficiency are

10

sound as elucidated in subsequent discussions of this publication. The spirit of eco-efficiency is expressed in Agenda 21, acknoledging that *"g(G) rowing recognition of the importance of addressing consumption has also not yet been matched by an understanding of its implications"* (Agenda 21, 1992). At the 2002 World Summit on Sustainable Development (WSSD) the Johannesburg Plan of Implementation (JPOI) affirmed the need to pursue eco-efficiency since *"global sustainable development depends upon fundamental changes in the way societies produce and consume"* (JPOI 2002).

This call for change resonated once more at the Fifth Ministerial Conference on Environment and Development in Asia and the Pacific held in March 2005 in Seoul, Republic of Korea. In the Meetings' Ministerial Declaration, 52 countries in the region endorsed the Seoul Initiative on Environmentally Sustainable Economic Growth (Green Growth) where one of its key targets is the improvement of eco-efficiency for environmental sustainability. Green Growth is an approach that seeks to harmonize the two imperatives of economic growth and environment sustainability by promoting fundamental changes in the way societies produce and consume resources. The notion calls for systematic changes in the outlook and view of development wherein societies, in general, needs to realize the inextricable links between social, environmental and economic aspects; environmental protection should no longer be viewed as a constraint to economic growth but instead is a primary driver of growth and essential for long-term sustainability; and production and consumption processes must be viewed not as a linear process but from a holistic/life cycle/circular patterns. Central to the promotion of green growth is the adoption of the principles of eco-efficiency, an approach that is directed towards de-linking economic growth with environmental degradation.

1.4 Scope of this publication

With the Ministerial Declaration at the Fifth Ministerial Conference on Environment and Development in Asia and the Pacific providing the basis, this publication focuses particularly on eco-efficiency and advocates for a new paradigm for economic growth. As a recurring theme, the discussions highlight that the current planning approach highlights only on the economic efficiency based on market price. But market prices do not reflect the ecological price which thus results in the abuse of natural resources and the ecological inefficiency of the economic system. The publication deals with the need to close the gap between economic efficiency and eco-efficiency by internalizing the environmental

cost in the economic system. The Chairman of the Worldwatch Institute and former Vice President of ESSO Norway, Mr. Oystein Dahle captured in essence the value of closing the gap between the economic price and ecological price when he cited that "socialism collapsed because it did not allow prices to tell the economic truth. Capitalism may collapse because it does not allow prices to tell the ecological truth."

More specifically, this publication will take an overview of the different aspects of eco-efficiency, how it is implemented in the North-East Asian subregion and the prospects for its wider application. The experiences of countries in North-East Asia are worth looking in the context that the subregion is comprised of countries with different stages of economic development, and is in a good position for showing the applicability of the eco-efficiency approaches. For example, the subregion has two of the most developed economies in the world, Japan and the Republic of Korea which have taken different paths to economic growth. It would be interesting to raise the question for the other developing countries of North-East Asia as to which model of growth will they follow.

The discussions are roughly divided into five key chapters. Chapter 1 presents a broad overview of the situation and conditions that justifies the pursuit of an environmentally sustainable economic growth for the Asia-Pacific region through resource efficiency. Chapter 2 makes a discussion of the theoretical underpinnings of eco-efficiency. The section looks at the definition of eco-efficiency, its origins, and a number of the important concepts which are important in building greater understanding of eco-efficiency. The chapter also cites some documented examples of eco-efficiency at the corporation level thus, providing basis for its appeal in developing economy-wide eco-efficiency models. Chapter 3 presents the collective and individual ecological footprint of countries in North-East Asia; a backdrop that justifies the imperatives to pursue macro level eco-efficiency. Chapter 4 touches on the several initiatives for eco-efficiency as practiced in China, Japan and the Republic of Korea. These initiatives, while recognizing that much remains to be done, are good foundation for developing the macro-level eco-efficiency measures. Chapter 5 focuses on the way forward: actions and critical major steps needed for up-scaling the eco-efficiency initiatives in North-East Asia.

2. ECO-EFFICIENCY: MOVING TOWARDS SUSTAINABLE DEVELOPMENT

2.1 What is eco-efficiency?

Finding a generally acceptable definition of eco-efficiency that reflects the soundness of its principles, an agreed approach for its quantification and measurement, and the practicality and usefulness of its framework remains to be a major challenge in the search for its substantial contributions to sustainable development. The present overall efforts of defining the eco-efficiency approach is a "work in progress": however, its appeal as a pragmatic model for attaining environmental sustainability continues to be reinforced.

Proponents of the eco-efficiency model strongly believe that the first step towards sustainable development lies in achieving efficiency in the use of resources at both micro- and macro-levels. In its simplest form, eco-efficiency is the integration of economy, ecology, and efficiency. Conventional wisdom looks at environmental and economic issues as distinctly separate: the former as an outcome outside of the market structures. Such a view is now being debunked wherein environmental problems, like pollution when taken from an economic perspective, is a clear reflection of a market failure; an economic inefficiency and considered as a loss to society. Eco-efficiency seeks to address such losses by reducing the relative amounts of inputs per output, which means less resources are used for each product produced or consumed. A more precise concept of eco-efficiency, as cited by the World Business Council for Sustainable Development (WBCSD) in 1997, "*is increasing activities that create economic value while continuously reducing ecological impact and the use of natural resources* (De Simone and Popoff, 1997)". As mentioned, the definition of eco-efficiency is evolving and, often, can be sector-specific. At the Second Green Growth Policy Dialogue held in Beijing in 2006, Paul Ekins defined eco-efficiency as "*getting more value from resources and the environment* (Ekins, 2006)." The WBCSD adopted the definition as "*Eco-efficiency is achieved by the delivery of competitively priced goods and services that satisfy human needs and bring quality of life, while progressively reducing ecological impacts and resource intensity throughout the life cycle, to a level at least in line with the Earth's carrying capacity* (WBCSD, 2000)."

It is acknowledged that there are other definitions of eco-efficiency but a common thread in all of its interpretations is the wise use of resources. Whether viewed from the perspective of producers or consumers, eco-efficiency is about the reduction of society's ecological footprint, through an increase in overall productivityof resource use.

15

ESCAP, within the framework of Green Growth, defines eco-efficiency as *"a measurement of the impacts of economic activity and growth on a country's carrying capacity"*. A country's carrying capacity refers to the ability of that country's resources to sustain the population over time; meaning that economic growth is contingent upon the availability of resources. As many countries, particularly in North-East Asia, have limited resources, they must be aware of their own carrying capacity and promote policies to keep their growth within those limits. Eco-efficiency should help societies manage their economic activities by remaining within their carrying capacities. As the necessity of economic growth is crucial in addressing poverty in the region, it is clear that eco-efficiency is the appropriate pattern of economic growth.

2.1.1 Origins of eco-efficiency

The term eco-efficiency was first coined in 1991 by the Business Council on Sustainable Development (BCSD, now the WBCSD). Originally developed as a management philosophy to *"[foster] innovation and therefore growth and competitiveness,"* eco-efficiency is now viewed as a philosophy for all sectors of society (WBCSD, 2000). The concept of sustainable development arose in the 1970s, around the time of the birth of the modern environmental movement. It was envisioned as a global philosophy of development that governments should pursue for the future of their countries. Recognizing that the benefits of economic growth is for the general societal welfare and is not only directed towards accruing short-term profits for the private sector, the BCSD looked at the potential roles that the business sector could contribute in promoting sustainable development: through the pursuit of long-term profits by incorporating activities that respects the carrying capacity of the earth. Eco-efficiency, packaged in a set of concrete steps, was envisioned as one way business could be a part of sound economic development policies. Since its introduction in the early 1990s, eco-efficiency has evolved into other sectors and is increasingly embraced as the necessary direction for economic growth patterns.

Shortly after introducing the concept, the BCSD was asked to develop a document for the 1992 United Nations Conference on Environment and Development in Rio de Janeiro to explain the potential role of the private sector in pursuing sustainable development. In response, the BCSD presented a paper entitled "Changing Course", which discussed the concept and application of eco-efficiency as a tool for sustainable development; highlighting the long-term environmental and economic benefits that could be gained by changing production and consumption patterns. At the conclusion of the Rio Summit, eco-efficiency was officially adopted as a way for the business sector to implement Agenda 21.

The WBCSD suggests that the practical application of eco-efficiency for business is guided by seven elements: reducing material intensity, reducing energy intensity, reducing dispersion of toxic substances, enhancing recyclability, maximizing use of renewables, extending product durability, and increasing service intensity (WBCSD, 2000). These elements are linked to three broad objectives, which should be applied throughout all operations of a company: reducing the consumption of resources, reducing the impacts on the natural environment, and increasing the product or service value.

Eco-efficiency has been embraced by hundreds of companies, including 3M, Dow Chemicals, Toyota, BASF, etc. These leaders in corporate responsibility believe that eco-efficiency is simply good business. The lessons learned by the private sector through the implementation of this philosophy are important to consider when developing eco-efficiency policies at the macro-level. Some examples are provided later in this paper which is important for national governments to support, embrace and apply through domestic policies.

2.1.2 What should be the right level of resource efficiency: some concepts in eco-efficiency

Generally, when eco-efficiency is discussed, the question of "how much" resource efficiency is enough is often asked. While there is no specific formula for establishing eco-efficiency goals, there are a number of concepts that attempt to answer the question of "how much." Some of these concepts are highlighted below and can serve as guides for decision-makers in promoting eco-efficiency as national policy.

Factor Four

Factor Four means doing more with less, doubling wealth and halving resource use at the same time, thereby improving efficiency by a factor of four. Intended to serve as a decision-making tool for governments, businesses, and individuals interested in promoting sustainable development, Factor Four sets a goal for improving resource efficiency. The Wuppertal Institute, a leader in the Factor Four concept, believe that efficiency gains can be realized by utilizing natural resources more efficiently, *"either by generating more products, services and quality of life from the available resources, or by using less resources to maintain the same standard* (Wuppertal Institute, 2006)."* In order to make this happen, governments need to look at the challenge of resource efficiency holistically: addressing government policy, consumer behavior, private sector actions, and the role of civil society. Similarly, the following policy approaches will create Factor Four results (Weizsaecker, 1997):

- Least-cost planning;
- Utility regulatory reform;
- Creating energy rebate markets;
- Correcting perverse incentives;
- Making better choices in the transport sector;
- Real-cost pricing, e.g. the inclusion of all costs when setting prices for products and services (social, environmental, etc.);
- Feebates;
- Ecological tax reform;
- Harmonizing international standards.

These approaches can help achieve the results envisioned in two additional resource efficiency concepts, Factor 10 and decoupling. It is important to note that the Factor Four concept addresses both production and consumption patterns. Without changing both sides of economic activity (e.g. production and consumption), growth patterns will not lead to significant shifts enough to ensure sustainable development. Potential efficiency gains can be harnessed in all sectors of society, with the most gains to be found in addressing energy, material, and transport production and consumption patterns.

Factor 10

Factor 10 focuses more on the reduction of resource consumption, and thereby the ecological footprint of a given economy. The concept moves beyond Factor Four suggesting that developed countries need to reduce resource use tenfold in order to truly be sustainable, i.e. current economies find ways of producing equivalent outputs with about 10 per cent of the current consumption rate of resources. Proponent of the concept believe that, at the current rates of extraction for production and consumption, a scarcity of resources will eventually lead to increases in costs of production resulting from higher commodity prices. This, in turn, will lead to declining rates of economic growth and higher rates of environmental pressure, thus causing downward pressures on the economy.

In order to reduce the current consumption rate of resources, the following policy options can be taken, in addition to those suggested under the Factor Four concept (Schmidt-Bleek, 1999):

- Recycling and reuse initiatives;
- Developing internationally compatible indicators that reflect the relative resource intensity of goods and services;

- Establishing green national accounting; and
- Shifting consumer behavior and perceptions of satisfaction.

While the discussions on Factor 10 mainly focus on the reduction of resource uses in developing countries, developing countries also should not ignore issues of resource consumption. There is a great opportunity to alter consumer behavior in developing countries as their standards of living rise through economic growth by establishing policies that set a framework for sustainable patterns of consumption, rather than waiting ten or twenty years and then trying to fix the problem of consumption.

Factor X

Factor X is similar to Factor Four and Factor 10: It measures and promotes the dematerialization of an economy. The higher the number for "X" is set, the higher the target is for the level of eco-efficiency. There are various arguments on what level society should be striving for, and it is often agreed that each nation has different needs and should determine their factor based on their own requirements. The means to achieve established goals for eco-efficiency are any combination of the suggestions under Factor Four and Factor 10.

Decoupling

Decoupling has been identified as one of the OECD's five objectives in its Environmental Strategy for the First Decade of the 21st Century. Decoupling "refers to the relative growth rates of a pressure on the environment and of an economically relevant variable to which it is causally linked" and essentially means "breaking the link between 'environmental bads' and 'economic goods'" (OECD, 2002). Decoupling can occur in two forms: absolute decoupling, when the environmental pressure does not change or decreases while the driving force increases; and relative decoupling, when the growth rate of environmental pressure is positive but less than the rate of growth of human activity (figure 2.1) (ESCAP, 2005). Decoupling is often viewed as the appropriate target for ensuring sustainable, long-term economic development and environmental sustainability in society.

Resource efficiency, resource intensity, and resource productivity

One may note in the previous discussions the concepts of resource efficiency, resource intensity and resource productivity are assumed to be understood which in essence are all measures of resource use and the economic value-added. Resource efficiency at its most basic definition means the "use of smaller amounts of physical resources in

Figure 2.1: Decoupling environmental impact from economic/human activity

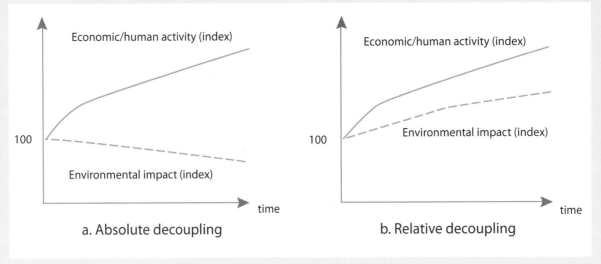

a. Absolute decoupling   b. Relative decoupling

Source: ESCAP, State of the Environment in Asia and the Pacific 2005, ESCAP

producing a unit of output" (NCSL, 1996). Resource efficiency is commonly measured as a ratio between useful material output and material input, which is also similar to the economic concept of efficiency. Resource intensity (or the material use intensity) looks at the "consumption of primary and secondary materials per unit of real Gross Domestic Product (GDP) which is calculated for one commodity at the country level". Its measurement is intended to document total material consumption trends as well as changes in the consumption patterns, which could bring close the measurement of the real material absorption of the economy (UNDESA, 2004). Both resource efficiency and resource intensity measure the ratios of resource use to the economic value-added. Resource productivity is the inverse ratio of the resource intensity as it "measures the efficiency with which the economy generates added value from the use of natural resources or the economic output or value added per unit of resource use or waste produced" (Gross and Foxon, 2003), e.g. GDP per ton of solid waste generated. Targets established under these concepts can be similarly achieved by the policy suggestions cited in the earlier sections.

2.1.3 Measuring eco-efficiency: developing the appropriate indicators

Critical to the discussions of eco-efficiency is the issue of what appropriate indicators can be used or developed that reflects eco-efficiency is indeed being attained. Without such measure how can the effectiveness of policies be determined? At the moment there is no consensus on how eco-efficiency indicators should be developed, much less, what

kind information should be collected for measuring the eco-efficiency of a product, enterprise, or of a society wide economic activity. Most of the eco-efficiency indicators developed currently focus on the production side (which is helpful but its scope is partial since it covers only the outputs from individual firms) with very limited effort made on developing indicators for the consumption side (which is a foundation for developing economy wide indicators). This gap offers opportunities for the refinement of indicator formulation process with the end view of defining measurable eco-efficiency markers that are applicable to every level of economic activities.

In this context how can a decision-maker really know that policies and actions are leading to greater eco-efficiency in society as a whole? By recognizing that the process is evolving, current eco-efficiency indicators can be complemented by existing tools and theoretical works for reviewing choices in pursuing sustainability (Enrenfield, 2005). A number of indicators for environmental performance exist, such as the Environmental Sustainability Index (ESI) and the Environmental Performance Index (EPI). The ESI benchmarks the ability of countries in protecting their environment (environmental stewardship) over the next several decades and allows for a comparative analysis of the policies relating to environmental systems, environmental stresses, human vulnerability to environmental stresses, societal and institutional capacity to respond to environmental challenges and global stewardship (Esty, Levy and others, 2005). The EPI measures two broad environmental protection objectives: reducing environmental stresses on human health and promoting ecosystem vitality and sound natural resource management (Esty, Levy and others, 2006). But certain caveats are stressed: these indicators are not sufficient in measuring the efficiency with which resources are utilized and therefore do not offer any prediction on the long-term economic development and environmental sustainability. Other indicators that could be helpful to decision-makers and are good building blocks for measuring the overall eco-efficiency of economic activities are that of UNCTAD eco-efficiency indicators, and the potential eco-efficiency indicators from ESCAP as discussed below:

↘ The United National Conference on Trade and Development (UNCTAD) has developed a set of guidelines for enterprise who wish to develop eco-efficiency indicators as part of their annual accounting. An indicator for eco-efficiency is the "ratio between and environmental and a financial variable. It measures the environmental performance of an enterprise with respect to its financial performance" (UNCTAD, 2004). They are promoting the inclusion of an eco-efficiency framework in corporate's annual reporting and believe that eco-efficiency reporting will be beneficial to business for the following reasons:

- Provide information;
- Improve decision-making;
- Complement financial statements (UNCTAD, 2004).

Combined with annual planning, eco-efficiency indicators can help improve the performance and competitiveness of firms, both environmentally and financially. UNCTAD guidelines offer specific tools for measuring a firm's activities at the macro-level, rather than at the product level, which would be too costly and time-consuming for most firms to implement. They target the water use, energy use, global warming contribution, ozone-depleting substances, and waste of any given enterprise. For each of these areas, UNCTAD presents a methodology for calculating, recognizing, measuring, and disclosing the following five indicators:

- Water consumption per net value added;
- Global warming contribution per unit of net value added (table 2.1);
- Energy requirement per unit of net value added;
- Dependency on ozone-depleting substances per unit of net value added;
- Waste generated per unit of net value added (UNCTAD, 2004).

As UNCTAD recognizes that countries have their respective unique characteristics they further encourage firms to develop additional indicators that will suit their specific needs, region, site, etc. using the guidelines provided. While the proposed indicators are directed for use at the firm level, the

Table 2.1: Eco-efficiency indicators of UNCTAD for global warming

CO_2 emissions related to energy use	Energy Requirement			Global warming contribution (100 y)	
	2001	2002		2001	2002
Electricity (Germany)	10 000 000	11 000 000	MWh	4 980 000	5 478 000 (t CO_2)
Electricity (Switzerland)	20 000 000	25 000 000	MWh	40 000	50 000 (t CO_2)
Natural gas (dry)	1 700	2 000	GJ	95 370 000	112 200 000 (t CO_2)
Bituminous coal	2 000	2 200	GJ	189 200 000	208 120 000 (t CO_2)
Motor gasoline	500	600	GJ	34 650 000	41 580 000 (t CO_2)
Energy derived global warming contribution				**324 240 000**	**367 428 000 (t CO2)**
Other greenhouse gases	2001	2002	Global Warming Potential (GWP) Kg CO_2 –eq./kg		
Sulphur hexafluoride (t)	3 000	2 800	22 600	67 800 000	63 280 000 (t CO_2-eq)
Other gases				67 800 000	63 280 000 (t CO_2-eq)
Total global warming contribution				392 040 000	430 708 000 (t CO_2-eq)
Net value added				**10 000 000**	**11 000 000 (€)**
Eco-efficiency indicator "global warming contribution/net value added"				**39.204**	**39.155 (t CO2-eq/€)**

Source: "UNCTAD. A Manual for the Preparers and Users of Eco-efficiency Indicators" version 1.1 2004

suggested tools and data for measurement can be used by governments to develop indicators for overall economic activity, broken down by sector, if desired. By collecting more specific data, governments will be able to determine appropriate targets and direct eco-efficiency policies where they will have the most impact.

Following these guidelines will help policymakers in developing an overall eco-efficiency strategy for the national economy.

↘ ESCAP State of Environment 2005 publication identified some potential eco-efficiency indicators, which examine resource use intensity, resource productivity, environmental impact intensity, pressure on carrying capacity, and the rate of resource savings of benefit accumulation (figure 2.5). As a follow-through ESCAP with support from the Republic of Korea has been working to further developing the indicators that captures the eco-efficiency of both production and consumption. ESCAP eco-efficiency indicators seeks to better understand the ecological pattern of economic growth. As observed, the prevailing economic development model is being driven by economic efficiency based on market prices and one that do not reflect the ecological costs. This is one major short fall of the present economic model. By focusing only on economic efficiency based on market prices, it does not internalize ecological costs that results to resource over exploitation and unbridled pollution. ESCAP key thrust is in improving the eco-efficiency of economic growth by identifying the means that will close the gap between ecological efficiency and economic efficiency. At the concluded Expert Group Meeting on Developing Eco-Efficiency Indicators of Economic Growth held in January 2007, a preliminary list of potential eco-efficiency indicators was identified (table 2.2). The meeting further recommended the following as basis for future work on the eco-efficiency indicators:

- Eco-efficiency indicators will be a set of indicators for a few sectors of economic activity;

- Initial focus areas shall be on energy, water, household consumption, land transport, urbanization, other infrastructure (e.g. residential buildings), other consumption indicators, other production indicators and other indicators relating to both consumption & production that can not be separated;

- Eco-efficiency indicators will link environment to economic activity at the national, urban and rural level;

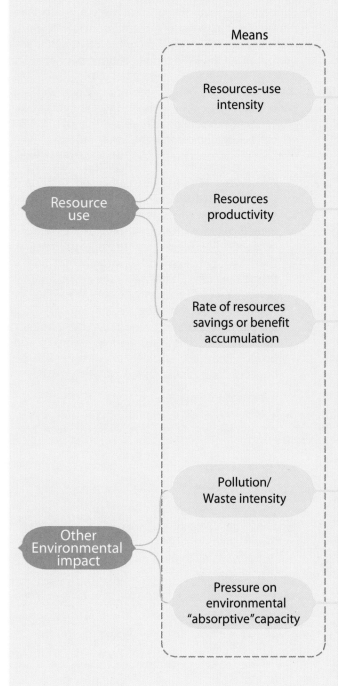

- Where possible, eco-efficiency indicators will address consumption and production separately, but for certain resources and sectors eco-efficiency indicators will address issues of consumption and production jointly;

- Eco-efficiency indicators will be measured in monetary and/or physical terms as appropriate;

- Some eco-efficiency indicators will be per GDP and others per capita;

Figure 2.2: Framework for developing eco-efficiency indicators of ESCAP

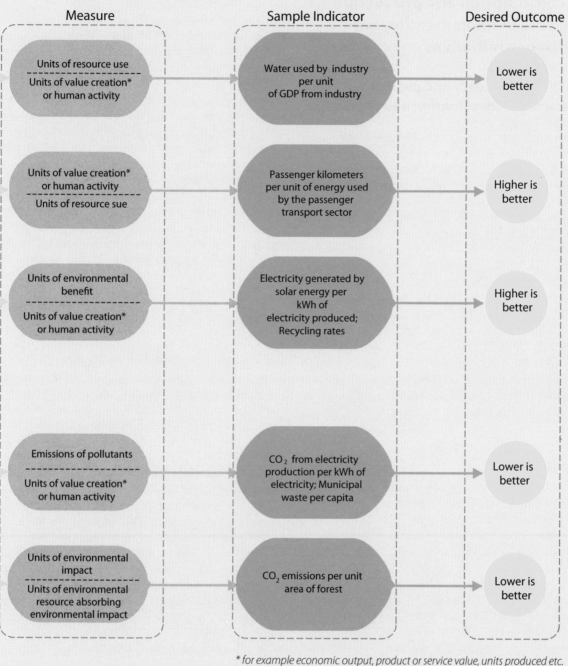

Measure	Sample Indicator	Desired Outcome
$\dfrac{\text{Units of resource use}}{\text{Units of value creation* or human activity}}$	Water used by industry per unit of GDP from industry	Lower is better
$\dfrac{\text{Units of value creation* or human activity}}{\text{Units of resource sue}}$	Passenger kilometers per unit of energy used by the passenger transport sector	Higher is better
$\dfrac{\text{Units of environmental benefit}}{\text{Units of value creation* or human activity}}$	Electricity generated by solar energy per kWh of electricity produced; Recycling rates	Higher is better
$\dfrac{\text{Emissions of pollutants}}{\text{Units of value creation* or human activity}}$	CO_2 from electricity production per kWh of electricity; Municipal waste per capita	Lower is better
$\dfrac{\text{Units of environmental impact}}{\text{Units of environmental resource absorbing environmental impact}}$	CO_2 emissions per unit area of forest	Lower is better

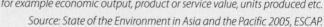

for example economic output, product or service value, units produced etc.

Source: State of the Environment in Asia and the Pacific 2005, ESCAP.

- Eco-efficiency indicators will be appropriate for the level of development and for the industrial structure of the economy;

- Relevant policy measures will be identified for each eco-efficiency indicators; and

- Technical issues including data quality and availability as well as simplicity will be used in selecting the indicators.

Once eco-efficiency indicators are established, a comprehensive view of the sustainability of a society or economy can be developed. Policymakers could choose from the basket of indicators available in an attempt to capture a realistic snapshot of the current state of sustainability in a given country (e.g. eco-efficiency indicators, ESI, EPI, human development index, etc).

2.2 Changing current patterns of consumption and production: the core of implementing eco-efficiency initiatives

2.2.1 Eco-efficiency and promoting sustainable consumption and production

Consumption and production patterns were long recognized to have significant bearing on sustainable development. Agenda 21, the programme of action for sustainable development, made clear stipulations for addressing the unsustainable patterns of production and consumption through the development of policies and strategies that would encourage change in these patterns. In 2002, the Johannesburg Plan of Implementation (JPOI) affirmed the same resolve, calling upon governments, international organizations, the private sector, and civil society and individuals to fundamentally change the way societies produce and consume (JPOI, 2002). The JPOI further elucidated the areas for which significant effort would have to be made in promoting sustainable consumption and production patterns, to wit: ten-year framework of programmes; cleaner production and eco-efficiency (see box 2.1); decision-making processes and corporate responsibility; energy; transport, waste and chemicals management.

Eco-efficient societies require dramatic shift in their current patterns of production and consumption. The idea of eco-efficiency stemmed from the evolving discussions of the environmental Kuznets curve (EKC) which hypothesized the relationship between environmental degradation and income per capita (Grossman and Krueger, 1995). Earlier discussions of the EKC theory argued that in the initial stages of economic growth environmental degradation and pollution correspondingly rises, but peaking at a certain income per capita level when the trend starts to reverse, so that further rise in income growth leads to an environmental improvement. Many development practitioners believe that the EKC has become the backbone of the current growth model of "growing up first and cleaning up later" (ESCAP, 2006). Over the years the theory has been the subject of review and empirical studies testing the validity of the relationship, applying varying methodologies in different types of economies. The review results were found to be mixed wherein some economies found that the EKC exists but do not necessary hold true for many of the environmental impacts (ESCAP, 2006). At the crux of the eco-efficiency discussions is in understanding the current patterns of production and consumption of societies and defining the policy

framework and parameters for which these patterns can be made more efficient.

The pursuit of eco-efficiency should be made in improving efficiencies in both production and consumption patterns. With the anticipated rise in incomes, production patterns of countries are also expected to improve with economic structures shifting to higher dependence on service-based and knowledge-intensive activities, and increasingly import, rather than produce, resource and pollution-intensive goods. But that is only one side of the formula. Improvements in income per capita can also spur conspicuous and discretionary consumption that could intensify the environmental pressures on the environment. Such trend can undermine the efficiency gains at the production side. The rapid expansion of urban centres in the subregion is already manifesting this pattern. Policymakers need to pay attention to these nuances as these issues can become entrenched in the growth patterns of the countries making the shift to eco-efficiency difficult to achieve.

Eco-efficiency of production patterns

Present efforts on eco-efficiency are notably led by the private sector in particular the major industrial players. Industry leadership is understandable given the imperatives for which they have to improve their efficiency in resource and material use. In general, the adoption of eco-efficiency principles in the production patterns can be immediate inasmuch as the drivers for shifts can be mandated by policies and/or are market response to a particular stimuli i.e. cost-effectiveness of compliance, technology improvements and responses to consumer behaviour or demand. Moreover, the strategic environmental value of adopting eco-efficiency in the production process strengthens the market position of the companies fortifying their competitive edge over other players that have not adopted the process (Cramer, 1998). Efficiency in production process has been the defining factor since the first industrial revolution and many argue that eco-efficiency is part of the evolutionary continuum of the early industrialization (McDonough and Braungart, 1998). Over the past two decades significant progress have been attained in improving the manufacturing technologies for existing and newly designed process, optimizing the consumption of raw materials and energy and also minimizing the environmental impacts. The perspective of eco-efficiency in the production process has also broadened over the years expanding to include environmental improvements of the products covering the entire lifecycle. Examples of eco-efficiency of the production process is further articulated and discussed in the latter sections (see

Box 2.1: Chapter 3 of the Johannesburg Plan of Implementation: Changing Unsustainable Patterns of Consumption and Production

Ten-year framework of programmes

A ten-year framework of programmes will support regional and national initiatives to accelerate shift towards sustainable consumption and production. This will promote social and economic development within the carrying capacity of ecosystems by addressing the delinking of economic growth and environmental degradation and mobilizing resources to help build capacity in developing countries. Actions needed at all levels include:

- Identifying specific tools, policies, and measures, including life cycle analysis and indicators for measuring progress [15a];

- Adopting relevant policies and measures that follow the 'polluter pays' principle [15b];

- Developing policies to improve products and services while reducing environmental and health impacts [15c];

- Raising awareness on the importance of sustainable production and consumption [15d];

- Employing voluntary consumer information tools [15e]; and

- Developing financial resources to increase eco-efficiency through capacity-building, technology transfer and the exchange of technology [15f].

Cleaner production and eco-efficiency

Increasing investment in cleaner production and eco-efficiency requires incentives, support schemes and policies that establish necessary regulatory, financial and legal frameworks [16]. Actions include:

- Establishing cleaner production programmes and centres, and particularly assisting small and medium-sized enterprises (SMEs) to improve productivity [16a];

- Creating incentives for investment in cleaner production and eco-efficiency [16b];

- Providing information on cost-effective examples and best practices [16c]; and

- Providing training programmes to SMEs about the use of information and communication technologies [16d].

Source: Plan of Implementation of the World Summit on Sustainable Development, available at www.un.org/esa/sustdev/ documents/WSSD_POI_PD/English/WSSD_PlanImpl.pdf

section 2.3 below). But at this point it is important to stress that the dramatic improvement in the efficiency of industrial process provide the backbone for upscaling the eco-efficiency philosophy at the macro-economic level.

Eco-efficiency of consumption patterns

Although eco-efficiency for production are steps in the right direction, these efforts however, are not sufficient in ensuring overall eco-efficiency. Equal attention would also have to be made to ensure eco-efficiency of the consumption patterns. The achievements gained through improvement of eco-efficiency in production patterns can be overwhelmed by continued expansion of unsustainable consumption patterns. The historical experience of the relationship between technology development and resource consumption testifies that past gains in efficiency in several areas (e.g. in the energy and transport sector) have been outstripped by absolute growth in the volume consumed.

But promoting eco-efficiency in the consumption patterns presents, more complex challenges than the initiatives for improving efficiency for production. The approaches will need to understand the factors that push consumers to behave in a particular pattern. Targeting policies and specific programme of actions that stress voluntary actions through education and market incentives are important but it would need macro-level consumption policies that would ensure eco-efficiency is comprehensively pursued. Macro-level polices can cover as much ground with the objective of influencing consumer behaviour in the choice of their actions. For example, infrastructure policies that underscore eco-efficiency can promote investments for efficient transportation systems. Instead of constructing more roads and highways which induce consumer to use individualized vehicles, investments can be made on interconnected mass public transport systems which can bring more people to particular destinations. This initiative can also be complemented by market based regulations such as the levying of higher taxes for larger cars, imposition of road-users tax or congestion charges.

Policies motivating individuals to take environmentally-friendly choices into account for consumption are inarguably key drivers in promoting eco-efficiency. However, voluntary changes of lifestyles to less material and less pollution intensity are also very necessary. Generally, voluntary changes are likely determined by the level of social acceptability of the need for changes. Social acceptability is based on the characteristic of society's culture in interpreting the connection between nature and human, and the value of consumption.

Thus, one of the key objectives for promoting sustainable consumption pattern is to expand environmentally conscious consumption cultures. Many societies of Asia, in fact, contain the cultures that are mostly inherited from traditional ethical approaches to nature and society, while societies are also rapidly transforming into western-style consumer societies. Having recognized the cultural virtue in the North-East Asian region, it is very necessary to reappraise the relations between the traditional approaches and sustainable consumption pattern. However, it does not mean to revitalize simply the traditional approaches as they were, since the socio-economic bases of the cultures are more thoroughly changing. It means a creative development of hybrid cultures of consumption combining the concept and practice of eco-efficiency with environmentally-friendly cultures as well as traditional ethics in relations to nature (figure 2.3).

Furthermore, individual's choice to adopt environmentally-friendly lifestyles should not be simply left to individual's self-awareness and self-determination. Individual's lifestyles have a strong *path-dependence* aspect to society's existing socioeconomic systems. For example, existing transportation infrastructure significantly shapes the scope of individual freedom in choosing modes of transportation. Without regard to efficiency, existing system tends to become a standard, imposing irreversible influence on individual's choice in various

goods and services. Thus, government's policies have critical power over voluntary changes of individual lifestyles as well as consumption culture of society. This aspect demands to take government's policies into serious consideration when cultural values and individual lifestyles are discussed in the context of consumption patterns.

2.3 Practices of eco-efficiency in the production side: Some firm-level examples

Early understanding of eco-efficiency was viewed as a business concept, "because it talks the language of business" (WBCSD, 2000). The WBCSD first introduced the concept in the early 1990s as a way to link the roles and responsibilities of business to sustainable development. In many of their publications and outreach materials, the WBCSD presents eco-efficiency as making good sense for business, because "being efficient is always a high priority for every company" (WBCSD, 2000). Their approach suggests that eco-efficiency should be applied to every area of activity within a company, "from eliminating risks and finding additional savings through to identifying opportunities and realizing them in the marketplace" (WBCSD, 2000). Integrating eco-efficiency throughout a business will provide financial savings and additional profits over the long-term. Additional incentives for private sector eco-efficiency come from financial markets, which are starting to place dollar values on leadership in sustainable development through such mechanisms as the Dow Jones Sustainability Group Index (DJSGI). These incentives from within and outside the private sector provide momentum for furthering eco-efficiency efforts across economies and are based on countless success stories. Some of the leaders in eco-efficiency at the firm level include Toyota, Toshiba, and BASF, which efforts are described below. Their initiatives can offer some fresh ideas and insights for broadening the reach of eco-efficiency at the macro-level.

Toyota

Toyota is a global leader in corporate responsibility and eco-efficiency. In 1992, Toyota summarized its management philosophy, which considers many social and environmental issues, in a document entitled "Guiding Principles at Toyota". Principle 3 speaks about eco-efficiency, to wit:

> "[We] dedicate ourselves to providing clean and safe products and to enhancing the quality of life everywhere through all our activities" (Toyota, 2005).

Figure 2.3: Emerging Asian consumerism pattern: when East meets West

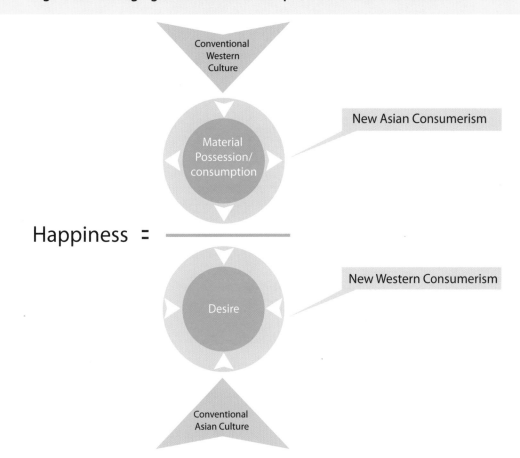

Source: Chung, Rae Kwon (2006). Presentation made at the First Policy Consultation Forum, Seoul Initiative Network on Green Growth, 6 -8 September 2006, Seoul.

Figure 2.4: Toyota's production process: Tracking resources inputs and substances released into the environment

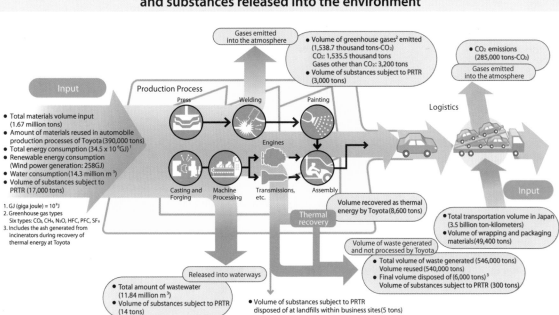

Source: Toyota Environmental and Social Report 2005.

Figure 2.5: BASF eco-efficiency analysis

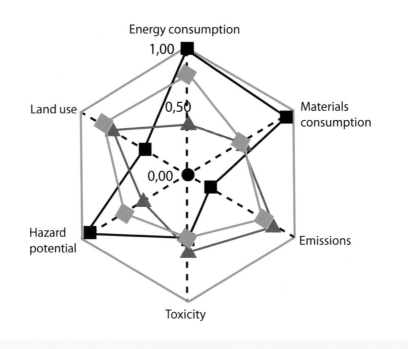

Source: BASF The Chemical Company <www.corporate.basf.com>.

By combining production goals with a quality of life goal, Toyota captured the interdependency of resource use with societal welfare; a premise upon which eco-efficiency is based. Economies use resources to improve the standards of living of societies. Toyota actualizes its sustainable production principle through its environmental management plans and community outreach. Using an approach founded on environmental values, Toyota enhances competitiveness and improves their eco-efficiency through investments and continuous performance monitoring.

Among its environmental goals, Toyota seeks to contribute to the building of a recycling-based society in Japan (*see Chapter IV for Japan's 3R programme*). This will be accomplished, in part, through a key component of their eco-efficiency policy: capturing material flow, which tracks all of the inputs and subsequent outputs of their production processes all the way to the consumer (figure 2.4). Toyota's success in achieving eco-efficiency over the last 14 years amounts to a 60 per cent increase in efficiency of CO_2 emissions and a 210 per cent increase in waste reduction efficiency. In 2004 alone, Toyota estimates a 121.9 million yen savings in energy costs (US$1.04 million). The company promotes investment in new technologies that can help reduce their environmental impact while at the same time introducing cost-savings or enhancing profitability of their products.

BASF

BASF, a German-based chemicals firm, prioritizes eco-efficiency as an important strategic management tool. Two of its six core values reflect the importance of eco-efficiency in its operations: sustainable profitable performance and safety, health, and environmental responsibility.

BASF believes that "the efficient use of resources is a basic economic principle" and that eco-efficiency is "a major financial strength and at the same time provides environmental advantages" (BASF, 2005). One of its most important contributions to eco-efficiency is its Eco-efficiency Analysis, developed to measure the performance of individual products and product systems. The analysis is used to measure total costs and environmental impacts at the product level up to system-wide levels, and includes cradle-to-grave impacts.[1] BASF looks at the following aspects of production and includes their measurements in their eco-efficiency analysis: energy consumption, land use, hazard potential, toxicity, emissions, and materials consumption (figure 2.5). BASF applies the analysis in order to use the least amount of resources possible, and produce a minimal environmental

---

1 Cradle to grave refers to a product's life cycle, including all of the products and processes that were made by another manufacturer and provided as an input into the final product.

impact while at the same time aiming to produce products that help consumers conserve resources. Recently, BASF introduced a label to identify those products which have undergone the analysis, including third party review. The label is valid for three years at which point the product must undergo another review to ensure continued compliance.

Toshiba

Toshiba, as part of its corporate philosophy, implements voluntary environmental plans every five years. One of Toshiba's goals is to design environmentally conscious products (ECPs) which take resource saving, reuse and recycling, energy savings, and reduction of toxic substances into consideration. The goal is to have 80 out of 100 products meet the ECP guidelines. Toshiba's pursuit of eco-efficiency is qualified by Factor T, a unique measurement to evaluate the performance of Toshiba products against earlier versions of the same products. Eco-efficiency is calculated by dividing the "value" of a product by the product's "environmental impact"; eco-efficiency is considered greater with a smaller environmental impact and a greater value. The factor is then determined by dividing the eco-efficiency of a product subject to assessment by the eco-efficiency of a benchmark product (Toshiba, 2006). Toshiba's aim is to improve product eco-efficiency in 2010 by 2.2 times (in 2004 average product eco-efficiency was improved by 1.36 times). The firm believes that through continued design efforts and improvements a goal of 2.2 gains in eco-efficiency is easily attainable.

Each of the above firms has demonstrated innovation, commitment, and success in making eco-efficiency a reality. The techniques developed to enhance production systems can be replicated at other firms, but it is the shift in attitude of governments incorporating the principles cited which can help promote eco-efficiency at the macro-level.

2.4 Eco-efficiency and rebound effects

One of the possible unintended consequences of eco-efficiency policies is the rebound effect. Rebound effects are, in essence, the loss of potential efficiency gains when a gain in resource efficiency corresponds with a lesser improvement in resource use. For example, the invention of compact fluorescent light bulbs was intended to address energy consumption and waste generation by providing consumers with a bulb that consumed less energy and had a much longer life span than traditional incandescent and fluorescent light bulbs. Combined with public

information campaigns, these energy-saving light bulbs were widely embraced by consumers in many countries of the world. One side-effect of the bulbs, however, was that more bulbs were being installed and consumers started using the bulbs for longer periods of time, or would leave them on even if no one was using the light. The increased consumption of bulbs and energy diminished the impact of the original intent of the policy, leaving society at about the same level of environmental impact as before.

Rebound effects can be direct or indirect. For example, as transportation becomes more efficient both in terms of time and cost, more people will travel, and those that travel will travel further and more often. This aggregate increase in total consumption of resources with a relative decoupling in production characterizes direct rebound effects. Indirect effects occur when faster transportation uses more fuel, which in turn puts more pressure on the environment (Jalas and others, 2001). Macro level rebound effects, e.g. economy-wide and transnational effects, occur when price or technology changes alter consumer preferences (Hertwich, 2005). For example, if energy efficiency reduces the demand of fuel to the point where the fuel price goes down, then consumption of energy will likely increase as a result of the lower price. Additionally, when a consumer is saving money on transportation, it is important to know where the saved money will be spent. If that money is being spent to purchase new appliances for the home, which require increased energy consumption, the net effect could be negative. Innovation can change the patterns of consumption, but it does not necessarily mean that new pattern has less environmental impact than the original pattern.

The potential for a rebound effect makes it imperative that any national policies relating to eco-efficiency focus on the producer and consumers sides of economic activity. Policymakers should strive to account for potential rebound effects when developing eco-efficiency policies by adopting a circular view of the economy. While it may be too arduous to tackle all probable rebound effects, governments should try to as much as possible anticipate these effects and try to offset them through other measures.

2.5 Expanding eco-efficiency efforts from firm levels to the macro-level

A recurring message stressed in this paper is that eco-efficiency at the firm level is not sufficient in alleviating the ever mounting pressures on the natural capital. The critical involvement of the private sector is undoubtedly crucial. However, eco-efficiency should necessarily be up-scaled at the macro level if the objective of sustainability is for the entire society to benefit. Hence, North-East Asia needs a comprehensive, holistic approach to build eco-efficient economies that will help eradicate poverty and reduce environmental impacts over the long-term. There needs to be a fundamental shift in the economic patterns of growth, which means changing the way the consumers and producers behave. The private sector alone cannot accomplish this, but it has offered a good starting point for national governments to move forward in developing the necessary climates for sustainable production and consumption.

One of the greatest challenges for sustainable development and eco-efficiency lies in the varying patterns of economic growth. It has been generally observed that as incomes go up, the eco-efficiency of production increases. Conversely, it has been noted that as income increases, the eco-efficiency of consumption decreases. This is somewhat discussed in terms of a rebound effect, but not in its entirety. In order to stabilize the patterns of growth and increase eco-efficiency of both production and consumption at the same time, a macro-level approach is needed. The key for governments is in providing the right conditions for the eco-efficiency patterns of economic growth to change, become sustainable, and remain within the biocapacity of the country or region. Through policy measures such as, among others, promoting more equitable access to resources, using demand-side approaches apart from supply-side interventions, and promoting cultural values and indigenous knowledge, governments can promote shifts in economic growth patterns towards eco-efficient economic growth.

The necessity for the macro-level approach is demonstrated when considering the challenges of energy consumption and climate change. While it is easy to regulate and "clean-up" production, it is much more difficult to appeal to consumers to change their consumption patterns.

3. ECO-EFFICIENCY AND SOCIETY: CASES IN NORTH-EAST ASIAN COUNTRIES

3.1 Economic growth and environmental sustainability

North-East Asia has experienced robust economic growth rates over the past forty years forging it as one of the biggest market in the world. Barring any major economic upheaval, this pattern of growth is envisaged to be maintained with projections indicating that the subregion is expected to assume 20 per cent of world economic strength in the next two decades (table 3.1).

Table 3.1: Economic Proportions of Selected North-East Asia Countries in the World Economy

(unit: per cent)

Countries and areas	2000	2005	2006-2020
Republic of Korea	1.6	1.8	2.2
China	3.6	4.4	5.8
Japan	12.7	11.8	10.9
Hong Kong, China	0.5	0.6	0.6
North-East Asia	18.4	18.6	19.5

Source: Mizuho Research Institute, Economic Outlook, 2004.

However, concomitant with the impressive economic growth were natural resource depletion and environmental degradation in some areas of the subregion. Unfortunately, this situation is projected to persist in the foreseeable future as urban population in North-East Asia is predicted to grow at an average rate of 2.4 per cent per annum between 2001 and 2040.

Central to discussions on the economic growth and sustainability issue is the pattern of consumption of natural resources. The first report that flagged consumption patterns would be a key issue that needs to be monitored given its inextricable links with sustainability and economic growth was the World Wide Fund for Nature (WWF) Living Planet Report of 1998. The report highlighted the fact that global consumption pressures are growing rapidly, which is exceeding the ability of the planet to replenish its natural resources. For the economies of North-East Asia the report shows that the per capita consumption and the aggregate national pressure on the environment for North-East Asia economies like China, Japan and the Republic of Korea, have ranked top among all countries in the Asia-Pacific (WWF, 1998). Consumers in Japan and the Republic of Korea have caused two times more pressure per capita to the environment than that of the world average. The per capita pressure for developed economies as Japan and the Republic of Korea has foreshadowed the trend of China in the near future. With her huge population and rapid pace of urbanization, China's continuing high GDP growth will pose even more intense pressure to the natural environment, if the unsustainable production and consumption patterns remain unchanged. Meanwhile, along with economic growth, subregional demand for natural resources is increasing at an unprecedented rate. Rocketing prices of oil and other key raw materials in the global market have rendered secure resource (energy in particular) supply and its efficient utilization cornerstone of national economy (table 3.2).

Table 3.2: North-East Asian countries' final energy demand by 2020

Country	1999 (in Mtoe)	2010 (in Mtoe)	2020 (in Mtoe)
Republic of Korea	125	190	250
Japan	342	376	409
China	768	1,024	1,353
Total	1,235	1,590	2,012

Source: APERC, APEC Energy Demand and Supply Outlook, 2002

3.2 North-East Asia's ecological footprint

North-East Asian economies significantly rely on natural resources and the environment to fuel their growth. The subregions ecological footprint and biocapacity provides a glimpse into the sustainability of current economic activity and trends for the future. The World Wildlife Fund for Nature (WWF), in their Asia-Pacific 2005: the Ecological Footprint and Natural Wealth report estimates that global demand for resources is "exceeding the Earth's regenerative capacity by more than 20 per cent" (WWF, 2005). With almost one-quarter of the world's population living in North-East Asia, the region will play an important role in "addressing overshoot as the region's population and economy continue to grow in a world with limited resources" (WWF, 2005). North-East Asia can make choices now to address its ecological deficit and help lower the global ecological deficit.

Currently, North-East Asia has an ecological footprint of 2.8 hectares per person, 30 per cent above the global average. The ecological capacity for the region, excluding Mongolia (its low population density contributes to a large biocapacity) is 1.9 hectares per person. The resulting ecological deficit is 0.9 global hectares per person: implying that the present demand on North-East Asia's natural capital is being spent faster than its rate of regeneration (figure 3.1).

Apart from having this deficit, some countries in the region have also been exporting its biocapacity to other parts of the world. A clear case is that of China's increasingly becoming the global manufacturing centre producing most of the manufactured goods consumed elsewhere in the world. To support its rapid growth, China has become the largest consumer and producer of commodities: it is now the second largest consumer of primary energy after the United States, the top global producer of coal steel, cement and 10 different kinds of ferrous minerals. Becoming the global manufacturing centre has also caused a dramatic surge in the demand for natural resources from oil, steel and other ferrous minerals consequently replacing United States as the dominant market and major price setter for these commodities (Hanson and Martin, 2006).

Figure 3.1: Consumption per capita and pressures in North-East Asian countries (2006)

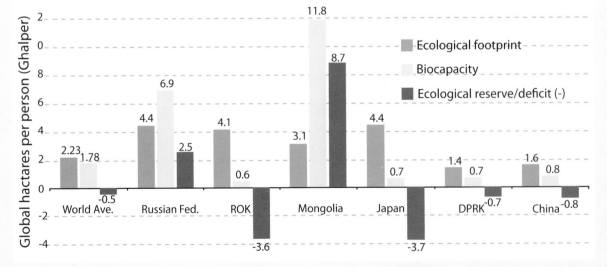

Source: WWF Living Planet Report 2006.

Hidden from these impressive expansions is the fact the all the residuals (waste and pollution) of the manufacturing processes are also left behind in the county producing the commodities, shouldering the brunt of environmental impacts and giving them the burden to clean up or rehabilitate their degraded natural environment.

Somehow lending credence to this pattern is the Environmental Performance Index (EPI), another set of environmental indicators advocated by the Yale University and Columbia University, when applied in the North-East Asian countries (table 3.3). Thus, the scenario for North-East Asian countries is unmistakable: unless economic growth is decoupled from environmental resource use, their ecological footprint will continue to increase while their carrying capacity steadily decreases.

In order to reduce the gap between the ecological footprint and biocapacity WWF suggests four factors that need to be considered viz.:

• Increase or, at a minimum, maintain biocapacity by protecting soil from erosion and degradation, preserving cropland for agriculture, protecting watersheds to secure freshwater supplies, maintaining healthy forests and fisheries, reducing contributions to global warming, and eliminating the use of toxic chemicals that degrade the environment;

• Continuing to improve resource efficiency through production;

• Cutting consumption of goods and services per person, especially for wealthy persons who would suffer no decline in quality of life by lowering their consumption; and

• Address population growth issues. A large population increases the ecological footprint of a nation, and reducing the population through measures that support families choosing to have fewer children will help to maintain the biocapacity of a country (WWF, 2005).

3.3 Imperatives for eco-efficiency in North-East Asia

The imperatives for North-East Asian economies to pursue a sustainable pattern of economic growth have never been more pressing than now. As

Table 3.3: Selected environmental performance Index for North-East Asian countries

	Indicators	China	Japan	Mongolia	Republic of Korea	Russian Federation
	Overall EPI Score	56.2	81.9	48.8	75.2	77.5
	Overall Rank	94	14	115	42	32
	Performance on selected indicators based on standardized proximity to target at (100=target met)					
Policy Category: Environmental health	Percentage with access to drinking water	58.5	100	31.4	85.6	92.8
	Percentage with access to adequate sanitation	31.9	100	50.2	100	84.2
	Urban particulates	44.7	83.5	56.9	76.8	88.88
	Nitrogen loading in milligrams per liter nitrogen in water bodies	35.0	99.8	–	99.2	99.7
Water resources	Water consumption, percentage of territory with oversubscribed water resources	64.3	89.7	79.4	82.3	96.2
Prod. natural resources	Timber harvesting, percentage of standing forests	98.7	100	100	100	100
	Overfishing	0	0	0	16.7	50
Sustainable energy	Energy efficiency (in terrajoules per million US$GDP (PPP)	77.3	80.8	20.2	67.5	12.8
	Renewable energy (percentage of total energy consumption	6.3	6.2	0	0.7	6.1
	CO_2 per GDP (emission per GDP (PPP)	36.0	95.0	0	83.6	20

Source: Yale University (2006). Pilot 2006 Environnemental Performance Index accessed on 20 January 2007 from <www.yale.edu/epi/2006EPI_Report_Full.pdf>.

countries are eyeing greater participation in the economic globalization process North-East Asian economies are projected to aggressively pursue a path for high economic growth. This pattern however comes with a stiff environmental price. With the exception perhaps for Japan, other countries in the subregion are pursuing growth models that entail increasing costs of environmental degradation, including costs related to the loss of environmental services, e.g. wetlands providing natural filtration for drinking water, forests providing carbon sequestration, etc. For example, recent estimates from China suggest that around 4 per cent of its GDP is lost annually to environmental degradation (SEPA, 2006).

North-East Asia also faces the more fundamental challenge to maintaining its phase of economic growth: resource availability. An examination of the subregion's carrying capacity all point to the direction that its natural capital (natural resource endowment) under the present modality of resource use would not be able sustain its growth in the long run. The constraints in their natural resources have also driven North-East Asian economies quest their raw materials for manufacturing products to meet both domestic demand and for exports from other countries in the Asia-Pacific region. The increased appetite for commodities is driving the global demand for resources such as oil, steel, ferrous and non-ferrous minerals, wood and wood products and others. Not only do these increased demand are jacking up the price for these commodities but in some certain ways it is also encouraging the exploitation of resources from the other developing countries outside the region (also termed as an ecological shadow). Unless the countries of North-East Asia, particularly the developing ones, start to shift to become eco-efficient, the current pattern can undermine the very base of their economic growth. North-East Asian economies is left with no better alternative for averting their unsustainable pattern of growth but to improve their ecological efficiency (or eco-efficiency).

3.3.1 Areas of focus for eco-efficiency: reflecting diversity in North-East Asia

The economies of North-East Asia are diverse. Developing countries of the subregion raises a fundamental question as to which model(s) of development is suitable for them. Even the two developed economies of the subregion, Japan (GDP/capita at PPP (2004) US$29,900) and the Republic of Korea (GDP/capita at PPP (2004) US$21,305), have exhibited different patterns of growth. Japan, in its early stages of industrial development, has extensively used natural resources, importing almost all of raw materials to fuel its growth. But Japan has also made a dramatic shift in their production and consumption patterns in the 1970's to become more resource efficient. The Republic of Korea, on the other hand, has patterned its growth with the United States model, which production and consumption patterns are not necessarily resource efficient. This pattern is manifested by looking at the footprint change per person of countries wherein the Republic of Korea has shown even higher footprint changes per person at 148 per cent than the United States (38 per cent) and Japan (30 per cent) for the period 1975-2003. In the same manner, the Republic of Korea's biocapacity change per person (-35 per cent) is also higher than the United States (-20 per cent) and Japan (-16 per cent). As the two are considered leading countries in North-East Asia it would be interesting to note which pattern of growth will China, the Democratic People's Republic of Korea, the Russian Federation and Mongolia will pursue as they aspire to also rapidly develop in the future.

The push for economic growth, high and rising incomes, urbanization, and changing lifestyles have triggered relatively high energy intensities in some countries, which may be symptomatic of declining environmental sustainability and increasing pressure on the natural environment. The pressure is manifested on the condition of the environment as reflected by persistence of urban air pollution related to transportation emissions, acid rain, stressed freshwater supplies and biodiversity loss, and the impacts of climate change. Transitional economies of the Russian Federation and Mongolia have been additionally burdened with out-dated technologies and narrow economic bases. The Democratic People's Republic of Korea focuses on land management to increase the agricultural production and alleviate the impact of natural disaster.

Other pressure points are in the consumption of other natural resources. During the 1990s, China has consumed 7 per cent of the world mineral resources like nickel, iron ore and aluminum, but the consumption increased rose up to 20 per cent in 2003. It is estimated that by 2010, the consumption will be more than double-fold on the 2003 basis. According to the 2006 China Sustainable Development Strategy Report, among 59 countries, China's consumption of water accounts for 15.58 per cent of the global total; non-renewable energy 12.287 per cent; finished steel 26.63 per cent; cement 45.61 per cent; non-ferrous metals 19.12 per cent in 2003. China's 2005 GDP grew 10 times quicker than that in 1949, but the raw material consumption rate has increased up to 50 times more.

Recently, China's Academy of Sciences has developed a Resource and Environment Performance Index

Table 3.4: Key resource-saving indicators for selected countries

Country (2003)	Water/GDP	Non-renewable energy/GDP	Steel/GDP	Cement/GDP	Non-ferrous metals/GDP
China	4.022	3.127	6.776	11.607	4.866
Japan	0.230	0.432	0.705	0.380	0.579
Republic of Korea	0.425	1.287	3.126	1.956	2.740
Russian Federation	1.931	5.583	2.067	1.876	2.215

Source: 2006 China Sustainable Development Strategy Report

(REPI) to signal the eco-efficiency rate in GDP growth (see Section 4 for further discussions of the REPI). Among all countries in the subregion, China ranked the top in the consumption of five basic resources per unit GDP achieved in 2003, indicating the least saving intensity (table 3.4).

Given the above considerations the following discussions reflect the key areas in which eco-efficiency initiatives in North-East Asian countries would have to be examined:

Water resources and water use

Eco-efficiency in the use of water resources aims at minimizing human impacts on the quantity and quality of water resources while meeting the socioeconomic demands for water. In this context, many North-East Asian countries face significant challenges as water quality in many rivers and lakes does not meet the national standard and in turn poor water quality reduces the availability of water resources, which induces social tensions. As the quantity and quality of water resources are positively correlated, improving eco-efficiency in the water sector needs to simultaneously address both issues.

Some indicators of eco-efficiency in the water sector include water withdrawal rates, water consumption per capita and per unit of GDP, and water quality. In terms of per capita withdrawals for domestic purposes, NEASPEC countries consist of three different groups. China and Mongolia, 32.6 and 36

Figure 3.2: Water withdrawals by sector, North-East Asia

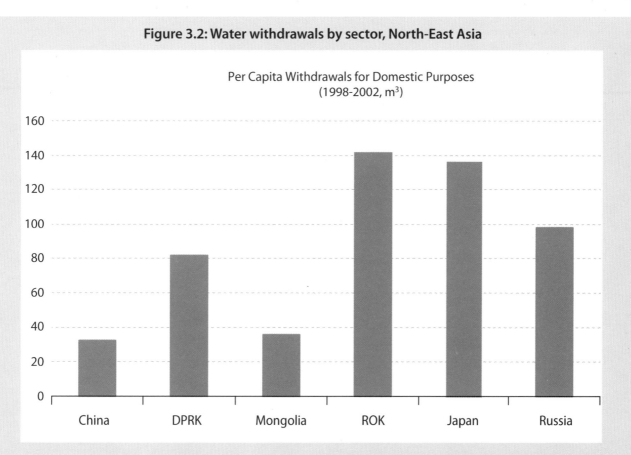

Per Capita Withdrawals for Domestic Purposes
(1998-2002, m³)

Source: ESCAP, Economic and Social Survey of Asia and the Pacific 2007.

cubic meters per capita, respectively, show the lowest levels of per capita consumption among NEASPEC countries while the per capita consumptions of Japan (137.0 m³) and Republic of Korea (141.6m³) are almost four times of the formers. The Democratic People's Republic of Korea (81.9 m³) and the Russian Federation (98.2 m³) are positioned in the middle. The substantially different levels of populations and national endowments of water resources provide countries with fundamentally different preconditions for eco-efficiency. Per capita water consumption is therefore limited as an indicator of a relative level of eco-efficiency between countries. Thus, such comparison needs to be supported by relating water consumption levels with economic activities as well as national trends relating to patterns of consumption.

The water consumption per unit of GDP (PPP-adjusted) in North-East Asian countries also shows significant disparities between countries. The Chinese Academy of Science's Resource and Environmental Performance Index (REPI), for example, shows the different levels of consumption intensity of water resources in relation to economic activity. The values of REPI for fresh water are 1.254 for China, 0.394 for Japan, 0.896 for Russia and 0.423 for the ROK. The world average serves as a bench mark with a REPI value of 1.00. The Chinese REPI value implies that producing per GDP in China requires 1.254 times more water than the world average. This also means that the efficiency of water use for per unit of GDP in China is about 80% of the world average. By contrast,

Japan and the Republic of Korea require less than a half of the world average. The performance of the two countries, however, cannot be simply translated as having an absolutely high level of eco-efficiency. The global situation of water resources is such that the world lacks eco-efficiency in water use and management. Thus, the relatively good performance of Japan and the ROK in comparison with the world average does not mean the achievement of eco-efficiency; there is still room for significant improvement.

Furthermore, improving the socioeconomic foundations for eco-efficiency in water use becomes more imperative in North-East Asia in a context of climate change. Climate change will impact on the distribution of water resources between geographic areas and increase existing socioeconomic vulnerability to the significant seasonal variations of water resources in most countries. The need to promote eco-efficiency in the use of water resources in this subregion is also quite compelling given its multiple users and anticipated expansion of demand due to increasing economic activity.

Energy resources and energy use

Energy supply and consumption demand generally defines the growth pattern of economies in the region. Historical comparisons in the subregion illustrate steep increase in total energy consumption in China, Japan and the Republic of Korea, steady increase but shrinkage in the Democratic People's Republic of Korea and the Russian Federation as

Table 3.5: Energy supply and consumption in North-East Asia

	Items	China	Democratic People's Republic of Korea	Japan	Republic of Korea	Russian Federation
Energy Supply	Total Primary Energy Supply (TPES) (Mtoe)					
	1990	866.52	32.87	445.97	92.65	
	2004	1,609.35	20.37	533.20	213.05	641.53
	TPES/capita (toe/capita)					
	1990	0.76	1.67	3.61	2.16	-
	2004	1.24	0.91	4.18	4.43	4.46
	TPES/GDP (toe per thousand 2000 US$ PPP)					
	1990	0.48	0.72	0.16	0.22	-
	2004	0.23	0.66	0.16	0.23	0.49
Energy consumption	Total Final Consumption (TFC) (Mtoe)					
	1990	481.71	26.32	305.60	63.98	-
	2004	819.22	16.52	354.32	143.69	422.55
	Electricity consumption/GDP (kWh per 2000 US$)					
	1990	1.31	1.61	0.19	0.36	-
	2004	1.20	1.76	0.21	0.58	2.47
	Electricity consumption/capita (kWh per capita)					
	1990	511	1,275	6,507	2,373	-
	2004	1,585	827	8,077	7,391	5,642

Sources: IEA 2006. Energy balances of OECD countries 2003-2004; and Energy balances of non-OECD countries 2003-2004 (Paris, OECD/IEA)

a result of economic sluggishness and downturn (table 3.5). The same table shows that in 2004 China ranked top in both energy supply and electricity consumption among all the North-East Asain countries; the Russian Federation had the highest rate of electricity consumption against GDP; Japan is first in per capita electricity consumption (IEA, 2006).

The current patterns of energy use of the economies of North-East Asia highlight two critical factors that provide compelling justification for the countries to adopt eco-efficiency measures. The first factor deals with sourcing of energy resources. All countries in the subregion are wholly or significantly dependent on imported oil to spur their economic activity. And this has significant implications in the pricing structures of the world oil market. China's case illustrates this point: between the periods 2000 to 2005 China accounted for about one quarter of the increase in world oil demand growth (Downs, 2006). According to the Asia Pacific Energy Research Centre (APERC, 2002), by 2020, the total energy demand of North-East Asian countries' will increase two times more than that in 1999, 70 per cent of is to meet China's demand alone. If China's annual economic

growth rate remains 6 per cent on the average till 2030, the country's primary energy consumption will accordingly rise from 0.85 billion tons to 2.4 billion tons. As the potential supply is 1.7 billion tons, the gap between the demand and the supply needs to be filled by import, which would cost about US$ 25.3 billion dollars. IEA estimated that, in 2025 (IEA, 2004), to meet the world's daily demand for petroleum, daily output of 21.5 million barrels would be required (table 3.6).

Japan's is another country in the subregion that is very much dependent on oil to drive its economy. From the mid-1950s to the end of the 1970s, Japan's economy shifted from reconstruction to a period of high growth. This transition led to major changes in Japanese lifestyles. At present, with a developed economy and highest per capita income among all North-East Asian countries, Japanese society is characterized by economic and social trend of mass production, mass consumption, and mass disposal. Figure 3.3 shows the energy composition of Japanese economy, which preponderantly relies on oil and other fossil fuels in transport and industrial sectors.

Table 3.6: Estimated petroleum imports among North-East Asian countries (2001-2025)

(million barrels/day)

	2001	2010	2015	2020	2025
Consumption	12.5	15.8	17.5	19.4	21.5
Republic of Korea	2.1	2.5	2.6	2.7	2.9
China	5.0	7.6	9.2	11.0	12.8
Japan	5.4	5.7	5.7	5.7	5.8
Import	9.2	12.2	14.0	15.9	18.1
percentage of Import	73.6	77.2	80.0	82.0	84.2

Source: IEA, World Energy Outlook, 2004.

Figure 3.3: Breakdown of sectoral final consumption by source in 1973 and 2003, Japan

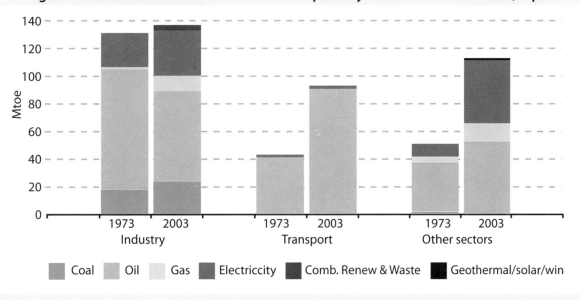

Includes residential, commercial and public services, agriculture and non-specified
Source: IEA, World Energy Outlook, 2004.

The Republic of Korea's per capita energy consumption and carbon emissions have increased dramatically over the past two decades. The country's per capita energy consumption has increased nearly four-fold, from 44.0 million Btu per person in 1980 to 170.2 million Btu per person in 2001. The Republic of Korea's per capita energy consumption was comparable to that of Japan (172.2 million Btu in 2001). Clearly, as demand for energy increases manifold countries would have to import these resources that results to thus raising the price of these commodities to point where it becomes costly.

The second factor that should impel countries to adopt eco-efficiency measures relates to emissions generated by fossil fuel based combustion systems to generate energy. Three major pollutants are key concerns for countries and the world: CO_2 which is precursor for global climate change, SO_2 and NO_2 which are known health hazards (table 3.7). Countries in North-East Asia are fully aware of the implications of unabated emission of the above pollutants and while command and control measures are being initiated to somewhat bring it down the recently reported successes can be negated unless complementary efforts are introduced that changes both the production and consumption behaviour of society.

Among the countries of North-East Asia which have shown dramatic reductions in the emission of SO_2 and NO_2 is Japan. The economic boom in the 1970s resulted in lowest efficiency in terms of per unit GDP levels of municipal waste, energy consumption and SO_2, CO_2 and PM emissions and severe environmental disasters. But with the raising of public awareness, enactment of environmental legislation, environmental institutional improvement and corporate society's participation in sharing environmental concerns, eco-efficiency of some selected indicators has greatly enhanced (figures 3.4 and 3.5). The drastic decrease of waste generation versus GDP is mainly attributed to the '3R' (reduce, reuse and recycle) strategy the government has been promoting since 1970s, following the enactment of the Waste Management Law. Further discussions will be made on the "3R Strategy" in the succeeding chapter.

A commonly used indicator for the measuring the pattern of energy use by countries is energy intensity per unit of GDP (ESCAP, 2006). Due to its importance in the pursuit of sustainability, the MDG has identified energy intensity as one of the indicators (Indicator 27) under Goal 7. Although there are theoretical misgivings for the use of this particular indicator, nevertheless countries committed to the attainment of the MDG have been measuring their respective energy use. According to the World Bank (United Nations, 2005), the energy intensity rate (apparent consumption; kg oil equivalent, per US$1,000 GDP/2000 PPP) released in 2005 shows marginal increase in the Republic of Korea from 1990 to 2002, while China dropped by 50 per cent

Table 3.7: CO_2, SO_2 and NO_2 emissions from fuel combustion in selected North-East Asian cities

Country	CO_2 (Million ton)		SO_2 (ug/m3)		NO_2 (ug/m3)	
	1995	2004	1995	2003	1995	2003
China	2,975.29	4,732.36				
- Shanghai	-	-	53	43	-	57
- Beijing	-	-		61	-	
Democratic People's Republic of Korea	74.74	70.2	-	-	-	-
Japan	1,140.4	1,214.99				
- Tokyo	-	-	20.94	10.47	63.97	54.66
Republic of Korea	361.42	462.1	-			
- Busan	-	-	60.20	26.18(2000)a		45.15
- Seoul	-	-	44.50	15.71 (2000)a	60.20	65.85 (2000)a
Russian Federation	1,588.9	1,528.79				
			WHO air quality guideline (1999) 50 (ug/m3)		WHO air quality guideline (1999) 40 (ug/m3)	

Sources: Clean Air Initiative Asia Secretariat, March 2005; WHO (2005). WHO air quality guidelines global update 2005; International Energy Agency (2006). CO2 emissions from fuel combustion 1971-2004 (Paris, OECD/IEA).

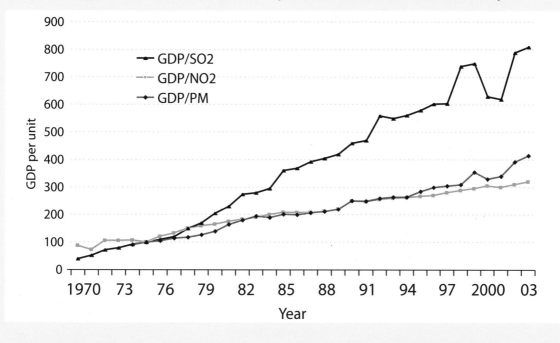

Figure 3.4: Trends of eco-efficiency of SO$_2$, NO$_x$ and PM emissions in Japan

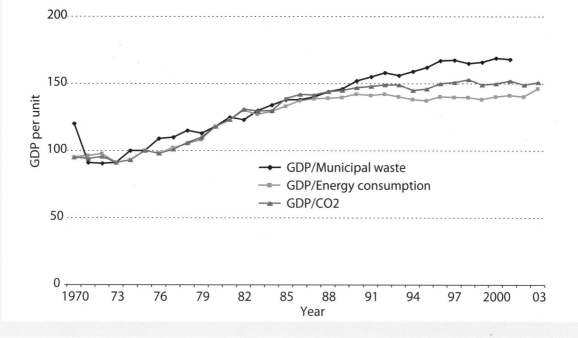

Figure 3.5: Trends of eco-efficiency of waste, energy consumption and CO$_2$ emissions in Japan

over the same time period. The Russian Federation's energy intensity in 2002 was one of the highest in the subregion, and was almost equivalent to China's 1990 level.

Energy intensity of the Russian Federation's economy had remained a key national economic problem ever since. The Russian Federation consumes over 0.5 kg of oil equivalent per dollar of GDP by purchasing power parity, compared to 0.1-0.2 kg in most of the industrialized and emerging economies (figure 3.6). Along with the Russian Federation in the high energy intensive 'club' are post-Soviet economies (Ukraine,

Kazakhstan). One of the graphs shows that such high energy intensity puts the Russian Federation in the same line of energy consumption per capita with the countries with GDP per capita (by PPP) 2-3 times higher, while for most of the emerging economies (which can be compared with the Russian Federation in terms of GDP per capita) energy consumption per capita remains very low. All this means that the Russian Federation's economy loses competitiveness due to the high energy consumption compared with other economies.

Figure 3.6: Comparative energy intensities of selected countries

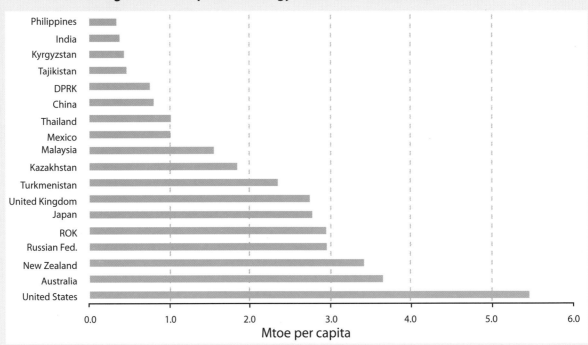

Mtoe per capita

Source: IEA Energy Balances of OECD Countries, 2003-2004, and Energy Balances of Non-OECD Countries, 2003-2004

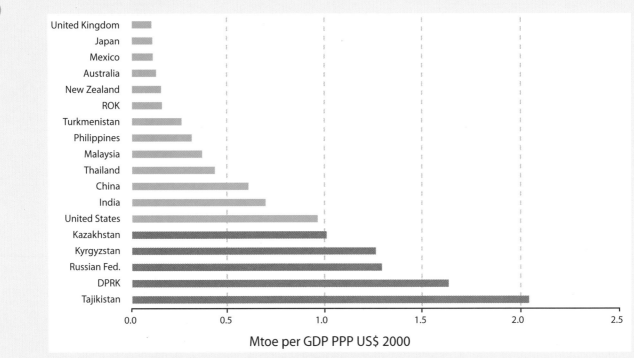

Mtoe per GDP PPP US$ 2000

Source: IEA, Energy Balances of OECD Countries, 2003-2004: and Energy Balances of No-OECD Countries, 2003-2004

Table 3.8: Trend of electric equipment production in China

(Unit: 100,000)

Items	1990	1995	2000	2001	Annual Growth Rate (per cent)
					1996-2001
Colored TV	1,033	2,058	4,154	4,187	12.6
Refrigerator	463	918	1,279	1349	6.6
Air conditioner	24	683	1,797	2,313	22.6
Washer	663	948	1,443	1,334	5.9
Electric range	-	200	1,281	1,818	44.5
Cell Phone	-	1,213	5,087	8,032	37.0

Source: Summary of Chinese Statistics, 2002

Discretionary consumption patterns

Inefficient energy use and unsustainable consumption pattern are becoming a major concerns in the subregion particularly by China and the Republic of Korea. In the case of China its rapid economic rise has also raised incomes per capita and households now have higher disposable incomes particularly in the urban areas. This trend has spurred the growing demand for durable consumer goods such as electronic appliances and other consumer products that represent a new found social status of being in the middle income brackets (table 3.8).

The same pattern of consumption is exhibited by consumers of the Republic of Korea. Purchase of bulky durable goods, such as home appliances is popular in the Republic of Korea. For instance, Korean consumers are 2.5 times likely to purchase large refrigerators than Japanese do, while the designed usefulness periods of these products are quite limited: refrigerator for 7 years, washer 6 years, color TV 7 years and automobiles at around 6.5 years (table 3.9). Compared with other OECD countries, the Republic of Korea is under high pressure from the consumption per capita, even though her income level is lower than that in OECD countries on the average. This unsustainable consumption occurred when per capita income was turning over US$10,000 as consumers are increasingly attracted to conspicuous and invidious consumption patterns.

For both China and the Republic of Korea this pattern has encouraged a consumption behaviour that increases energy use, low reuse and recycling rates that could pose a major obstacle for promoting eco-efficiency. The challenge is in defining macroeconomic policies that would somehow steer away consumers from following such unsustainable consumptive behaviour.

Motorization and transport infrastructure

Motorization rates and vehicle density are other indicators that are used in measuring the country's development (World Bank, 2004). Both measures while generally indicate mobility of population as influenced by economic policies and cultural preferences also reflect the consumption behaviour and the transport infrastructure investments made by governments. In the subregion both the developed and developing economies exhibit particular trends for the motorization of their societies. Significantly dictating the pattern of motorization are the investments made in the transportation sector and in North-East Asia region the trajectory of transport investments appears to indicate that the pattern of motorization is leaning towards greater ecological inefficiency. For example, the boom in the demand for individualized vehicles has spawned increased consumerism which has negative implications to the environment. In China, the rise in the demand for individualized automobiles has amplified the potential of the transport sector to becoming a major source of air pollution in urban centres. In 2003, China has jumped to become the third ranked in the world, next only to the United States and Japan, in automobile demand. This suggests that for every

Table 3.9: Proportion of market share of imported goods in the Republic of Korea

(in per cent)

Products	1995	1996-1998	1999-2001	2002
Color TV (over 25 inch)	46.9	63.9	70.4	75.5
Refrigerator (over 500 liter)	35.2	55.0	43.8	50.3
Washer (over 8.6kg)	33.3	61.9	81.2	83.4

Table 3.10: Sales of domestic automobiles by size in Republic of Korea

(unit in '000)

Vehicle type (Engine size)	2001		2002		2003		2004		2005		2006p		2007p	
	Unit	%	Unit	%	Unit	%	Unit	%	Unit	%	Unit	%	Unit	%
Light (800 cc)	82	7.7	57	4.7	42	4.2	47	5.5	47	5.1	40	4.0	43	4.0
Small (800 -1599)	79	7.4	94	7.7	50	5.0	47	5.5	59	6.5	81	8.1	80	7.4
Midsize (1600-2000)	588	55.2	627	51.2	489	48.9	430	50.1	509	55.8	560	56.1	611	56.2
Large (>2001)	316	29.7	447	36.5	420	42.0	334	38.9	298	32.6	317	31.8	354	32.5
Total	1,065		1,225		1,001		858		913		998		1,088	

Source: Second Dialogue on Green Growth, 2006, Prof. Jong Ho Hong(Hanyang University), <http://www.greengrowth.org/download/15dec06/2.roundtableworkshop_Bangkok_Hong_final.ppt>

Table 3.11: Congestion cost of road transport in selected countries

Country	Congestion cost as percentage of GDP	Source and Year of estimates
Europe 17a	3 per cent	INFRAS/IWW (2004)
OECD countries	3 per cent	OECD (2001)
United States	1.5 per cent	OECD (2001)
Philippines (Manila)	4 per cent	Sigua and Tiglao (2000)
Thailand (Bangkok)	1-6 per cent	Lvovsky, K and others (1999); SweRead (1997); Pendakur (1996)
Japan	2 per cent	Ministry of Land, Infrastructure and Transport (2000)
Republic of Korea	2.97per cent	Korea Transport Institute (KOTI)(2005);

Note: a Europe 17 covers the countries of Austria, Belgium, Denmark, Finland, France, Germany, Greece, Ireland, Italy, Luxembourg, Netherlands, Norway, Portugal, Spain, Sweden, Switzerland and the United Kingdom.
Source: Information compiled by ESCAP ESDD (2007)

100 sets of automobile sold, 7.3 sets are purchased by the Chinese consumer (China Statistics, 2002). The type of cars preferred by Chinese consumers also indicates the need to promote eco-efficiency in the consumption patterns. In 2004, 72 per cent of cars with above 2000cc engine capacity, which are considered to be less efficient, were sold in China.

The Republic of Korea similarly exhibits such skewed behaviour towards individualized motorization. Consumer preference for larger cars also defines the pattern of automobile acquisition in the Republic of Korea. Light vehicles with 1,000cc engine capacity or below that are known to be more efficient accounts only for 3.9 per cent of the total auto output as compared to Japan produces (and sells in the market) about 22.6 per cent (table 3.10).

While consumption behaviour is a significant factor for pursuing eco-efficiency initiatives in the transport sector, the pattern of transport infrastructure development equally plays a critical role in promoting the concept (ESCAP, 2006). As generally observed in the subregion, the rates of increase of vehicles on the road do not match the increases in the transport infrastructures such as the road networks. For the periods 1997-2003 the following North-East Asian countries had these motorization rates (number of private cars per 1,000): Japan – 334.2; the Republic of Korea - 171; the Russian Federation - 146.2 and China – 7. And between the periods 1993-2002 road network growth in Japan, the Republic of Korea and China grew by about 0.5 per cent, 5.1 per cent and 5.6 per cent respectively (ESCAP, 2005). In many of the urban centres of these countries, this situation has resulted to high road network densities, attendant traffic congestion, increased energy consumption and burgeoning air pollution. For example, in 2004, the Republic of Korea's vehicle density or number of vehicles per route kilometre is estimated at 150 as compared to Japan's 62. The congestion cost as percentage of GDP for the road transport between Japan and the Republic of Korea is estimated at 2 per cent and 2.97 per cent respectively (table 3.11). In the case of the Republic of Korea, it is particularly noteworthy that, the Seoul metropolitan area, a small part of the country, occupies 51.8 per cent (US$ 12 billion) of the national traffic congestion cost, causing the metropolitan area to become ecolomicaly and ecologically inefficient.

One alternative that presents opportunities for eco-efficiency initiatives is to shift the transport infrastructure investments to mass based systems such as railroads, subways and bus systems which carry more passengers. ESCAP reported that some significant investments are being made in this mode of transportation for a number of North-East Asian countries (ESCAP, 2005). These investments, while noted and encouraged, need to be expanded and aggressively pursued by governments. Simultaneously, governments would also have to explore policy inducements (market-based incentives and disincentives) to shift consumer behaviour preferences.

Special considerations for eco-efficiency in North-East Asia: cases for the Democratic People's Republic of Korea and Mongolia

a) Democratic People's Republic of Korea

The Democratic People's Republic of Korea is endowed with certain economic resources, including sizable deposits of coal, other minerals, and nonferrous metals. The river systems of the Aplot (Yalu), Tumen, and Taedong, and lesser rivers supplement the Democratic People's Republic of Korea's coal reserves and form an abundant source of hydro-power. Agriculture of the country concentrates on paddy rice cultivation in the coastal lowlands and corn, wheat, and soybeans grow on dry field plateaus. The country's hilly areas also provide for timber forests, livestock grazing, and orchards.

With slow economic recovery, the Democratic People's Republic of Korea's energy demand steadily climbed from 2000 on, despite the continuous fall from 1990 as a result of political difficulty and economic stagnation. This trend is expected to persist due to the following factors triggering the increase in energy consumption are:

- Modest residential energy demand increase;

- Certain extent of agricultural modernization (rising electricity consumption);

- Commercial sector floor space, electricity/coal use increase, partly because of transmission and distribution losses;

- Transport mildly increase;

- Increased industrial activities on the basis of high energy intensity of the industrial sectors.

An abundance of water resource has allowed the development of hydro-electric power network. Since the 1970s, the country has increasingly turned to coal as a key source. Thermal plants tend to be less efficient due to technological barriers, hence high environmental impacts. The fact that vegetal wastes form the basis of fuel consumption is indicative of the Democratic People's Republic of Korea's agriculture-dependent economy. The only oil-fired thermal plant is a 200-megawatt plant operated with crude petroleum imported from the Russian Federation.

In the Democratic People's Republic of Korea, the power sector's installed capacity is estimated at 11,000MW and split nearly evenly between coal fired and hydroelectric plants. The power plants and the transmission-distribution facilities are in serious need of rehabilitation, retrofitting and upgrading. Given its lack of foreign exchange and the domestic economy's poor conditions, the Democratic People's Republic of Korea lacks access to either technology or capital required to develop new energy sources, to improve energy efficiency and conservation, to rehabilitate its electricity transmission and distribution grid or to develop reliable local power generation plants. The country now faces the urgent need for clean coal combustion and exhaust gas purification technologies, energy efficiency, and renewable energy alternatives. In a nutshell, current lower level of energy consumption is largely due to the economic slowdown, but "the Democratic People's Republic of Korea's energy consumption is expected to double over 30 years, from almost 48 million tons of oil equivalent in 1990 to 96 million tons in 2020" (Kirby, 2006).

b) Mongolia

Mongolia is a large, land-locked, lightly populated country. Almost half of population is engaged in agriculture, particularly the uniquely Mongolian herding industry. The urban population is primarily located in the capital, Ulaanbaatar, and a few other large towns. Being one of the coldest and driest countries on earth, environmental regeneration in Mongolia is naturally slow, which accounts for the fragility of the environment. People's livelihood is highly dependent on natural resources.

Table 3.12: Fuel consumption and emission of CO_2 in Mongolia

Fuel Type	1990			2000		
	Combustion, (kt)	CO_2 Emission (kt)	SO_2 Emission (kt)	Combustion (kt)	CO_2 Emission (kt)	SO_2 Emission (kt)
Coal	6,654.0	9,604.9	33.20	5,185.0	7,000.0	25.9
Gasoline	541.2	1,731.9	1.56	272.1	871.0	0.8
Jet fuel	34.0	108.0		30.0	96.0	
Diesel	554.7	1,719.6	10.96	191.7	590.0	3.8
Residual fuel oil	63.4	183.9	0.36	30.6	90.0	0.15
Total	7,847.3	13,349.0	46.1	5,709.4	8,647.0	30.65

Note: CO_2 emissions from biomass fuels are not included in the calculations

Table 3.13: Some social indicators of herders in Mongolia

Indicators	1991	2000	2001
Number of herders	245,000	421.400	407,000
Number of herder households	114,000	191,000	185,500
Number of herder households with electricity	12,300	42,000	24,800
Number of wells	24,600	–	8,200

Source: National Statistical Office of Mongolia (2002), Mongolian Statistical Yearbook 2001. Ulaanbaatar, National Statistics Office of Mongolia.

44

The major industries are cashmere processing, copper and gold mining, food processing, and the construction materials. Agriculture accounts for close to 21.1 per cent of GDP, industry and construction for 43.9 per cent, and services for about 34.9 per cent (2006). Mining, mainly copper, provides an estimated 27 per cent of the economy's export earnings (1998). The industrial sector is one of the largest energy users, consuming about 70 per cent of the electricity and 30 per cent of the heat produced.

Coal is the major type of fossil fuel used in Mongolia. Natural gas is neither produced in Mongolia nor imported for domestic consumption. Oil products are imported and used for transport, power and heat plants.

During the 1990s, when the economy was in transition, energy production and combustion decreased sharply. However, electricity production was relatively stable in the same period. Between 95-97 per cent of electricity was generated by power plants and the rest by diesel generators in rural areas. The main reasons for the reduction of CO_2 emissions decrease were that the national industry came to a standstill and that energy combustion efficiency rate increased rapidly due to the Government's environmental initiatives and private investment in renovated facilities in large-scaled power plants. SO_2 emission was due to the decrepitude state of power plants, old automobiles and household use of coal for heating and cooking (table 3.12).

Energy costs in Mongolia are high because of the extreme climate and a legacy of inefficient use and wastage. Anywhere from 30 per cent to 50 per cent of local budgets are spent on heating schools, government buildings, libraries, health clinics and other public services. Therefore eco-efficiency in heating becomes the primary concern of the government.

Similarly, only 13.4 per cent of the herder's households were provided with electricity. Some 15.7 per cent of households possessed TV sets in 2001 (table 3.13). Rural areas in Mongolia are suffering from the so-called 'energy poverty' (Shagdar, 2003). Participatory Living Standards Assessment (PLSA) done by the Mongolia government in 2000 revealed that the number of poor and extremely poor households increased substantially during 1995-2000 (National Statistics Office of Mongolia and World Bank, 2001). In Mongolia, 70 per cent of all households, including urban and rural areas, had access to electricity at the end of 2000 and 85 per cent in 1990 (table 3.14).

Table 3.14: Electricity production and consumption in Mongolia

Indicators	1990	2001
Total resource, million kWh	3,576	3,213
Consumption, million kWh	2,719	1,948
- Agriculture, million kWh	116	17
- Communal housing, million kWh	349	476
Total population, million	2.0977	2.4425
- Urban population, million	1.1957	1.3971
- Rural population, million	0.902	1.0454
Electricity produced per capita, kWh	1,664.0	1,235.0
Electricity consumed per capita, kWh	948.7	797.5
Household electricity consumption per capita in urban areas, kWh	291.9	340.7
Household electricity consumption per capita in rural areas, kWh	128.6	16.3

Source: National Statistical Office of Mongolia (2001), (2002), Mongolian Statistical Yearbook 2000, 2001.
Ulaanbaatar, National Statistical Office of Mongolia.

Despite the fact that the final energy consumption per unit GDP dropped by 60MJ/US$, energy consumption in general remains on a high level due to the following two factors:

- Planned production regardless of quality or demand;

- Lack of economic incentives to reduce production costs, use of raw materials and energy.

To sum up, despite the steady increase in power demand (table 3.12), Mongolia remains low in energy efficiency and almost zero in renewable energy consumption.

4. NORTH-EAST ASIA ECO-EFFICIENCY INITIATIVES

4.1 Pursuing national eco-efficiency initiatives in North-East Asia

In 1992, the Rio Declaration and Agenda 21 adopted at United Nations Conference on Environment and Development proclaimed that states should reduce and eliminate unsustainable patterns of production and consumption to achieve sustain-able development. Ten years later, the Johannesburg Plan of Implementation encouraged countries to develop a ten-year framework of programmes to accelerate the shift towards sustainable consumption and production.

In response to their international commitment and national environmental pressure, North-East Asian countries have included comprehensive environmental initiatives for sustainable develop-ment in their national strategies and action plans such as China's Tenth Five-Year Plan for National Economic and Social Development (2001–2005), Mongolia's National Action Programme for Sustainable Development for the 21st Century (MAP-21) adopted in 1998, the Republic of Korea's Green Vision 21 (1995-2005) and National Environmental Vision for the New Millennium. Japan amended the Basic Environment Plan in 2000, but has also initiated several new policy frameworks aimed at reducing the resource intensity and waste production of the Japanese economy.

In the previous section, emphasis was laid on the energy efficiency of North-East Asian countries. To boost the all-round eco-efficiency both in production and consumption, governments of China and Japan are promoting Resource Efficient and Environment-Friendly Society (REEF Society) and Reduction of waste generation, Reuse and Recycling of resources and products strategy (3R Strategy). The following discussions present a sampling of national initiatives on eco-efficiency in the context of sustainable development as pursued by the countries of the North-East Asia.

4.2 China: Resource Efficient and Environment-Friendly (REEF) Society

To address the environmental impacts of high material and energy intensity, extensive toxic substance release, low recycling rate of per unit GDP, Chinese government started to make resource saving policy in the early 1980s. In 2005, the resource saving policy was promoted as a basic national development policy and included in the comprehensive Five-Year-Plan. Referred to as the Resource Efficient and Environment-Friendly (REEF) Society, it is

Figure 4.1: Basic structure of REEF: the essential elements of a resource-saving society

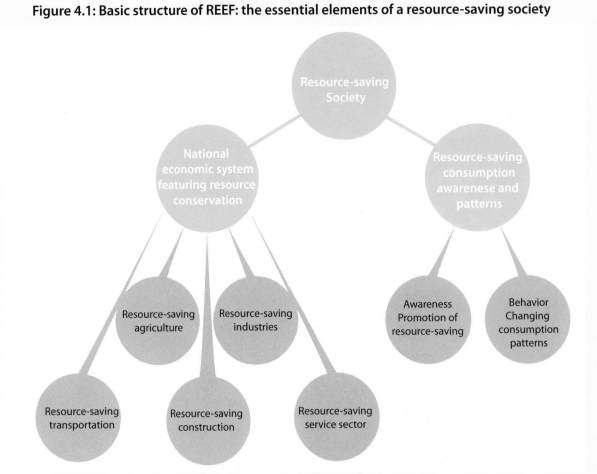

Box 4.1: Resource and Environmental Performance Index

REPI Definition

$$REPI_j = \frac{1}{n} \sum_i^n w_{ij} \frac{x_{ij}/g_j}{X_{i0}/G_0}$$

X_{ij}/g_j: the i th resource consumtion or pollutant discharge per unit of GDP of the j th coury or region;

X_{i0}/G_0: the i th resource consumption or pollutant discharge per unit GDP of the world or j th country

REPI j is the weighted average value of the ratio of selected resources consumption and pollutants discharge performance/intensity

REPI signifies:

The smaller the REPI value, the higher the resource productivity or eco-efficiency

- If REPI=1, Which indicates that i the respource and environmental performance of j th country or region equals to that of the world or j th country;
- If REPI>1, Which indicates that i th resource and environmental performance of j th country of region is smaller than that of the world or j the country;
- If REpi<1, Which indicates that i th resource and environmental performance of j th country or region is bigger than that of the world or j th country;

The same weight given to each resource and pollutant performance indicator

Source: Chinese Academy of Sciences, China Sustainable Development Strategy Report, 2006.

defined as 'conserving resources, improving utilization efficiency, sustainable economic growth with less resources in the process of production, construction, circulation, consumption, etc. by taking measures such as structural adjustment, technology improvement, enhanced management, further reform, promotion, etc. The current strategy of 'REEF Society' breaks down into two aspects: on the one hand, a wide range of integrated means will be applied to rationally relocate, recycle and reuse resources in a highly efficient manner at every point of production and consumption; on the other hand, pollutant generations and other environmental impacts of production and consumption will be minimized.

As the theoretical basis for proper policy making to implement the REEF strategy, the Chinese Academy of Science developed a composite indicator called the Resource and Environmental Performance Index (REPI) which intends to reflect, monitor and assess the progress of REEF at international, regional and industrial levels (box 4.1).

The calculation of REPI was applied to 59 countries' taking into account consumption of five key resources: non-renewable energy, fresh water, cement, non-ferrous metals and finished steel. Using the countries' 2003 GDP (both the market and PPP) as the denominator, an index is derived which represents the resource saving status of the countries. The REPI calculations of the 59 countries reveal the following results: using GDP at PPP, China ranks Fifty-fourth among all 59 countries; Japan has the best performance ranking Nineteenth; the Republic of Korea ranked the Fifty-fifth and the Russian Federation the Forty-fourth. In terms of GDP at market rates, Japan ranks Tenth, the Republic of Korea ranks Forty-second, the Russian Federation ranks Forty-eighth and China ranks Fifty-sixth. These

figures are quite alarming for China prompting the government to assess its current growth strategy. For instance, China's energy intensity has exceeded that of the developed nations by 120 per cent (table 4.1) particularly in some vital industries such as electricity, iron and steel production, non-ferrous metal extraction, petrochemical, light engineering and textile.

Historical studies of consumption levels of the five resources cited earlier and of chemical fertilizers, waste water discharge, emission of SO_2 and CO_2, industrial solid waste generated during 1980 and 2003 have shown gradual annual decreases in both pollutant emission and resource consumption by 5.6 per cent. This positive trend in the late 1990s is a reflection of economic restructuring and technological advances. However, the year 2003 saw a mild rebound in resource consumption levels and pollutant emissions as China's GDP boost is driven largely by the highly resource-intensive heavy-chemical industry (HCI).

At the country level, the research result reveals that GDP level negatively correlates to the resource saving status of a country. As a country is at the lower level of development, it is worse off in resource efficiency and environment performance than the wealthier, more developed states. In general, the turning point occurs at about per capita GDP US$3,000. Domestic analysis of the year 2003 shows similar trend: in the more economically developed coastal provinces, the resource intensity/GDP (PPP) is relatively lower than middle and western provinces, where the industries concentrate on mineral extraction and infrastructure construction, etc. and where the technological level in industrial production is relatively lower.

To redress the situation, the Eleventh-Five-Year Development Plan of China has pinned down the

Table 4.1: Comparison of resource and environmental performance index between China and group of 7 countries (G8), in 2003

Countries	REPI (GDP in US$)	China's REPI/G7's REPI (GDP in US$)	PEPI (GDP in PPP US$)	China's REPI/G7's REPI (GDP in PPP US$)
United Kingdom	0.282	21.6	0.446	4.3
France	0.390	15.6	0.588	3.2
Japan	0.465	13.1	0.796	2.4
United States	0.479	12.7	0.681	2.8
Germany	0.507	12.0	0.754	2.5
Italy	0.629	9.7	0.838	2.3
Canada	0.732	8.3	0.916	2.1
China	6.079	1.0	1.896	1.0

Source: Shaofeng Cheu, Chinese Academy of Sciences, May 2006

Figure 4.2: Changing Tendency of China's resource and environmental performance index from year 1983-2003

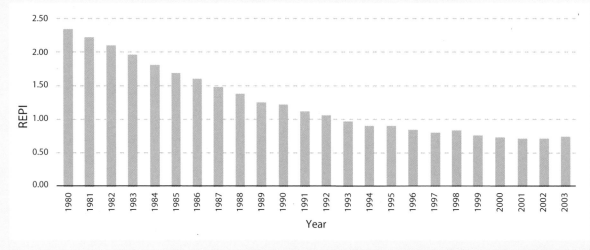

Source: Chinese Academy of Sciences, China Sustainable Development Strategy Report, 2006.

Figure 4.3: Relationship between resource and environmental performance index (GDP in US$) and per capita GDP (US$) in 59 countries (2003)

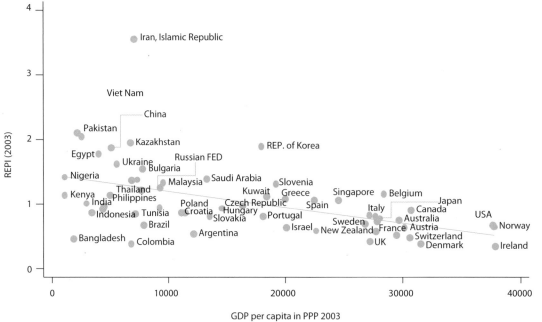

Source: Shaofeng Cheu, Chinese Academy of Sciences, May 2006

Table 4.2: China's resource-saving targets by 2020

Decreased Resource Use intensity (resource consumption per unit of GDP)		Decreasing pollution intensity (emission or discharge per unit of GDP)		Increasing recycling rates	
Energy	50-60%	SO$_2$ emissions	75%	Waste steel recycled	55%
Water	80%	CO$_2$ emissions	60%	Non-ferrous metal recycled	50%
Cement use	55%	Wastewater discharge	70%		
Steel and iron use	40%				
Non-ferrous metals use	20%				

Source: China Academy of Science

52

Table 4.3: China's strategic directions for a resource-saving society

Objectives	Strategies	
1. Resource saving growth	• Drive up growth by investments and exports.	• Pulling by consumption & investments, domestic demand and overseas demand.
	• Driving growth through industries.	• Pulling by industries, service sector and agriculture.
	• Driving growth by input of material essentials.	• Rely on technology improvements.
	• Pattern of growth: resource – product – waste - resource.	• Resource – product – waste – renewed resources.
2. Resource-saving industrial structure	• Develop service sector to increase share in the economy.	
	• Develop high-tech industries and information.	
	• Apply high technology to transform traditional industries.	
	• Phase out backward techniques, technologies and equipment.	
	• Reorganize enterprises and promote industries of scale.	
	• Adjust energy consumption structure and increase the share of high-quality energy.	
3. Resource saving urbanization	• Consider resources and environmental capacity in urbanization.	
	• Improve planning of construction zones and build green belts.	
	• Develop energy-saving buildings and centralize urban heating systems.	
	• Build an integrated transportation system featuring resource conservation.	
	• Save water in cities and promote intermediate water reuse.	
	• Regulate the recycling of renewable resources.	
4. Resource saving consumption	• Nurture consumption awareness: thrift and civilized.	
	• Nurture consumption pattern: resource-saving.	
	• Encourage the production and use of energy-saving, water saving and environmentally friendly products.	
	• Produce and use energy-saving and environmentally-friendly vehicles.	
	• Develop energy0saving buildings that occupy less land area.	

Source: China Academy of Science

national resource-saving targets by 2020 (compared to 2000 levels) (table 4.2):

In the mid-term, the targets boil down into 'by 2010, double fold GNP on the 2000 basis with optimized industrial structure, improved efficiency and reduced resource consumption; a 20 per cent reduction of resource consumption per unit GDP compared to that of the year 2000; checking the trends of ecological deterioration and drastic decrease of arable land. In achieving these targets, the plan outlined the strategic directions that will ensure the attainment of the targets (table 4.3).

Guided by these strategies, China has started to promote a people centered, well-coordinated, technology-oriented development path with supportive institutional public awareness building mechanisms. Table 4.4 specifies the microscopic strategies that are to be pursued under a resource-saving society. The guiding framework for achieving the microscopic strategies is also the macroscopic strategies which are articulated as follows:

Paradigm shift

• *Shift 1*: from 'end-of-pipe' strategy of pollution prevention in production to integrated process planning and control both in consumption and production so as to integrate resource efficiency and environmental protection into all economic activities, structural adjustment and environmental legislation process.

• *Shift 2*: from development's full reliance on natural resources and resource intensive models to reliance on human resources and technological innovation and information based development models.

• *Shift 3*: from segmented and sectorally divided environmental management model to integrated and well-coordinated environmental management with good governance.

53

Establishment of "Five-Support Systems" (development models)

- Building a national REEF production system, with emphasis on promoting industrialization by Information and Communication Technologies (ICT) application; replacing outdated technological processes and equipment by applying high and new technologies to upgrade traditional industries; giving priority to green manufacturing industries, information industry, service industry and sustainable agriculture; and promoting energy efficiency and increasing renewable resource consumption.

REEF urbanization model

- Establishing (a) compact city clusters to achieve economy of scale in resource use; (b) transit-oriented development model; (c) sustainable integrated urban public transport system; (d) green buildings and infrastructure building that economize the uses of land, energy, raw materials and water.

Sustainable consumption model

- Reviving traditional frugality values to guide consumption behaviors; public awareness raising among producers and consumers towards rational consumption; green consumption (opting for green products that are conducive to environmental protection and health); government being the role model to eradicate extravagant and imprudent consumption behaviors.

Resource-saving oriented technological innovations

- Self-reliant innovations and intellectual property right protection in resource exploitation, which concentrates on raising energy supply, replacing non-renewable by renewable resources, enhancing energy efficiency, reducing environmental impacts of resource uses; the establishment of integral management especially to promote the highly efficient uses of water, land, mineral and forest resources; promoting technological advances to control pollutant emissions, effluent, exhaust and soil erosion; the development of ecological monitoring technologies and environmentally friendly agriculture. Technologies of clean coal, renewable energy, hydrogen power and fuel cell as petroleum substitutes etc. are among the major innovations promoted.

Environmental institutional capacity building and legislative reinforcement

- The daunting task of overall REEF society construction places high requirements on the development visions, institutional basis, management systems and policymaking skills.

- Good governance, accountability and rational decision-making process serve as the cornerstone to materialize all the visions listed above.

- Resource-saving public sector and government serve as the role models for the rest of the population; Green procurement system is set up to cultivate REEF market for products, and green supply chain management system is set up to ensure the compliance to the environmental norms and standards by enterprises.

- Market force should be brought into full swing in raising the efficiency of resource allocating and utilization; A wide range of economic instruments should be employed to internalize the environment costs and to get the price right; Eco-tax, environmental auditing and eco-labeling systems should be established to provide incentives for resource-saving production and consumption; a market access system is needed to screen resource and energy intensive industries and products.

- Civil society organizations and mechanisms should be mobilized to assist in achieving the objectives.

- Policies and legislation need to be made to protect environmental property right.

- Resource-saving and environmental friendliness are two criteria to assess the performance of public administration.

- Uniform national environment standards should be set up for performance monitoring and evaluation.

- Environment regulations and laws need to be made, mandating environmental obligations for actors participating economic activities, i.e. extended producer responsibility system. Accordingly, law enforcement has to be strengthened to ensure the positive results.

- Society-wide environmental education programmes and campaigns to reshape consumption values are important means to guide the masses onto the path of sustainable consumption.

- A macro-environment conducive to human resource, knowledge and information development is created especially for the protection of intellectual property right.

To sum up, the core values of REEF society are 'saving', 'resource efficiency', 'pollutant discharge reduction' and 'environmentally sound treatment of wastes', with the priorities on saving energy, land, water materials, and circular economy. Methods to materialize these objectives lie in the adoption of comprehensive instruments including various institutional arrangements, structural adjustment and technology innovation etc.

Table 4.4: Microscopic strategies for pursuing resource-saving society

Energy Efficiency			Water	Material conservation	Land conservation	Resource conservation
Policy	Sector specific initiatives	Projects				
Strengthen energy label management, guide users & consumers to buy energy saving products & intensify corporate R&D for these products;	Industries: focus on high energy-consuming sectors and 1,000 enterprises (whose annual energy consumption over 10k tons);	Coal-burning Boiler (Kiln) Improvement Project	Promote water-saving irrigation & dry farming;	Enhance management on raw materials consumption in key industries;	Encourage intensive use & saving;	Integrated use of industrial waste;
Expand the certification for resource-saving products & seek international mutual recognition & exchange	Transportation: phase out old vehicles, enhance fuel standards, promote clean-fuel & put on pilot programmes of ethanol fuel;	Regional (Heat & Power) Cogeneration Project	Improve technologies in high water-consuming industries & utilize recycled water in industries;	Avoid over-packaging;	Amend & improve quota indices for construction land use;	Recycling renewable resources;
Enforce power demand side management, improve power use & increase end-use efficiency;	Buildings: enforce new energy-saving design standards & improve existing buildings;	Residual Heat & Pressure Utilization Project	Support seawater desalination;	Reduce and replace timber;	Promote organized land utilization in rural areas;	Integrated use of straws
Implement energy service contract to provide enterprises with services of diagnosis, designing, financing, improvement, operation & management;	Commercial & civil: expand energy conservation certification, enhance mandatory label management & implement "Green Lighting" Project;	Oil Conservation & Replacement Project	Enhance water saving & sewage recycling in cities;	Popularize bulk cement	Further curb farmland demolition for baking bricks	
Implement energy conservation voluntary agreement & encourage enterprises or industries to voluntarily achieve energy conservation targets;	Government organization: takes the lead in improving buildings & energy-consuming systems for conservation, buy energy and water-saving products & highlight conservation in decision-making;	Power Generators Energy Conservation Project	Develop & popularize water-saving equipment & utensils			
Implement government purchase of energy-saving products, expand the scope of water-& energy-saving items for purchase & lower the energy expenditure for government agencies.	Promote renewable resources: wind, solar & biomass energy, etc., develop marsh gas & coal-saving ovens in rural areas;	Energy System Optimization Project; Building Energy Conservation Project; Green Lights Project; Government organization Energy Conservation Project; Energy Conservation Monitoring and Technological Service System Construction Project				

4.3 Japan: The 3R initiative

The Western society in the 20th century featured socioeconomic activities based on mass production, mass consumption and mass disposal. Prevalent consumerism symbolizes material prosperity; however, it also implies increasing natural resource depletion and mounting waste generation that challenges the carrying capacity of nature (figure 4.4).

Japan underwent several decades of rapid economic growth after the Second World War. Soaring national income has triggered major changes in people's lifestyle at household level—from traditional frugality towards inclination to convenience and up-scaling lifestyle norms—manifested as 'newer' and 'more'. Ever-emerging new products and models owing to technological innovations render obsolete the current models so readily that regular landfills can hardly handle these 'wastes' with conventional methods. The limited national land for disposing these waste versus increasing domestic bulky trash and plastic waste, as well as hazardous industrial waste led to Japanese government's adamant legal and policy measures to tackle the issue of waste.

4.3.1 The 3R initiative

In the 1970s, Waste Management Law laid a foundation for further endeavors in 'pollution diet' and environmentally sound management of waste. The nation-wide '3R Initiative' (reduction of waste, increase reuse and recycling of resources) for a sound material cycle-society was officially launched by Japanese Prime Minister and adopted by G8 Meeting in 2004 as part of G8 Action Plan.

The sound circular economy model (sustainable model) shows a closed material use loop (figure 4.5); while the old paradigm has created an imbalance between resource input and waste discharge, which directly challenges the carrying capacity of nature. A comparison between the old model of material flow in modern economy and the sound circular economy reveals the sustainability of the latter, hence desirability for Japan, for its quite limited territory space.

The 3Rs serve as the guiding principles of production and consumption for the government, corporate and civil society to achieve the scenario switch (figure 4.6). The centerpiece of the initiative is that instead of being seen as things to be disposed of, waste is regarded as valuable resources for further use. The 3R Initiative is believed to bring multi-folded benefits the society: harmonizing environmental and economic concerns at the national level, minimizing waste at local level, serves as a driving force for increasing resource productivity and thus, competitiveness of industries and facilitates citizens' hands-on contribution to a better environment. Japan's waste management and recycling policy concentrates on three major areas:

Polluter Pays Principle

Responsibility of waste-generating businesses refers to the idea that waste-generating businesses should be responsible for treating its own waste through proper means as recycling, final disposal, etc. Under the 'Polluter Pays Principle', environmental load generators are obliged to take care of the environmental impacts of their production.

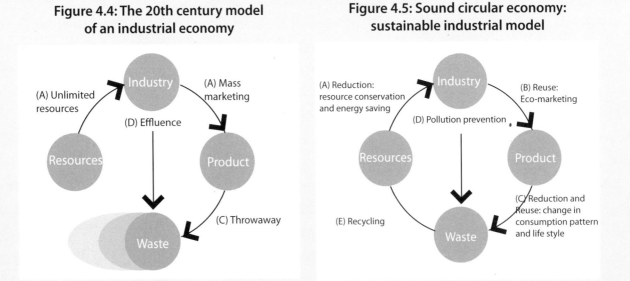

Figure 4.4: The 20th century model of an industrial economy

(A) Unlimited resources
Industry
(A) Mass marketing
(D) Effluence
Resources
Product
Waste
(C) Throwaway

Figure 4.5: Sound circular economy: sustainable industrial model

(A) Reduction: resource conservation and energy saving
Industry
(B) Reuse: Eco-marketing
(D) Pollution prevention
Resources
Product
(C) Reduction and Reuse: change in consumption pattern and life style
(E) Recycling
Waste

Figure 4.6: Conceptual framework of the 3Rs

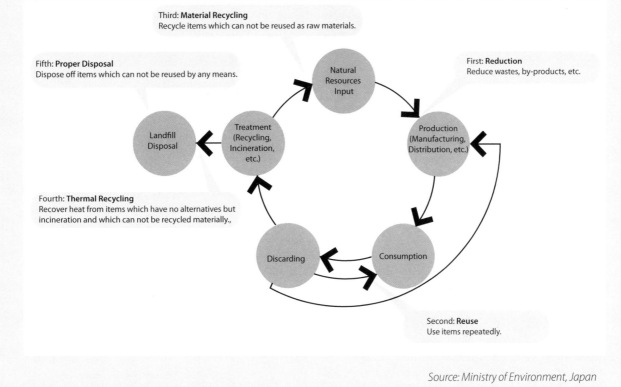

Third: **Material Recycling**
Recycle items which can not be reused as raw materials.

Fifth: **Proper Disposal**
Dispose off items which can not be reused by any means.

First: **Reduction**
Reduce wastes, by-products, etc.

Fourth: **Thermal Recycling**
Recover heat from items which have no alternatives but incineration and which can not be recycled materially.,

Second: **Reuse**
Use items repeatedly.

Source: Ministry of Environment, Japan

Strategy

Legal and institutional rules to regulate waste dumping and disposal under Polluter Pays Principle are (a) continuous revision of the Waste Management Law; (b) promotion of appropriate treatment through the reinforcement of regulations to prevent illegal dumping; and (c) eliminating adverse legacies under national leadership (disposal of PCB waste)

Extended Producer Responsibility (EPR)

An internationally shared concept, EPR is the extension of the responsibility of producers for the environmental impacts of their products across the product chain to the entire product life cycle -- and especially for their take-back, recycling, and disposal. Two important implications ensues the concept: (a) the shifting of responsibilities (physically and/ or economically; fully or partially) upstream to the producer and away from municipalities; and (b) providing incentives for producers to incorporate environmental consideration in the design of the products. The waste management responsibilities are therefore shifted from local authorities and general taxpayers to the producers. EPR can provide a pressure point to drive upstream changes in material selection and in the design aspects of a product. Appropriate signals can be sent to the producer to internalize substantial externalities from the final disposal of the product.

Four primary objectives underlie the concept of EPR:

(a) Source reduction (natural resource conservation/ material conservation);

(b) Waste prevention;

(c) Design of more environmentally compatible products;

(d) Closure of material use loops to promote sustainable development.

Instruments developed for producers embrace:

(a) Product take-back;

(b) Deposit/refund schemes;

(c) Material taxes, upstream combination tax/subsidy;

(d) Advance disposal/fees;

(e) Standards: minimum recycled content requirements; and

(f) Leasing/servicing.

Strategy

Based on the above recognition, the concept came to be discussed at OECD working group, who prepared and published a guidance manual for OECD member governments.

57

Domestically in Japan, the concept is clearly noted in the Fundamental Law for Establishing a Sound Material-Cycle Society. Along with legislation, Japan is setting up recycling systems for containers and packaging, household appliances, construction materials, food and vehicles, corresponding to the particular qualities of each product. With ten years of execution, the systems proved to have greatly boosted the recycling rate and encouraged businesses to reduce packaging, to recycle used home appliance, to engage in sorted demolition of construction waste and its recycling, to recycle food-related waste, and to recycle Freon, CFC, airbags and remnant materials after scrapping.

Decentralizing to municipal levels the management of waste

Stakeholder collaboration, especially collaboration between central and municipal governments, is considered as a key to bring optimal results. Promotion of Regional Plan for Establishing a Sound Material-Cycle Society (SMS) was approved by Ministry of Environment in 2005. In order to substantiate approaches towards the SMS at the local level, municipalities are required to build municipal waste treatment systems based on regional characteristics that cover waste reduction, sorted collection, recycling, heat recovery and final disposal. The Central government's roles lie in the preparation of guidelines to facilitate SMS implementation on the local level based on the Regional Fundamental Plans for Establishment of an SMS.

Technological advances[2] have an essential role to play in promoting approaches in line with the three aforementioned trends in waste management and recycling measures. But central to an effective waste management is lifestyle change[3] which calls for a reassessment of the inherent values with a sense of respect (Mottainai) to society[4].

4.3.2 Material flow indicators

Lately, Japan has been setting numerical targets under their Fundamental SMS Plan and making coherent efforts to effectively promote individual measures based on the plan. The Fundamental Plan for Establishing a Sound Material Cycle Society presents material flow in FY2000 and quantitative targets for three material flow indicators (i.e., input—resource productivity, cycle—cyclical use rate, and output—final disposal amount) for FY2010 which are set based on the FY2001 material flow (figure 4.7).

The Japan Ministry of the Environment announced the material flow and figures of three indicators for FY 2001 as follows:

Material flow

An overview of the material flow in FY2001 shows that 2,140 million tons of material was put and approximately 50 per cent or 1,120 million tons were accumulated in the form of buildings and social infrastructure, 120 million tons were exported, 400 million tons were consumed as energy, and 590 million tons were discharged as wastes. Out of the total amount discharged, 210 million tons were recycled.

Balance of material flow

To achieve sustainability, economic level of human activity within the limit of renewable resource supply and the assimilative capacity of natural ecosystem has to be optimized. Minimization of exploitation of natural resources and total wastes from anthropogenic sphere is accomplished only through holistic understanding, holistic restructuring and holistic management of material flow of anthropogenic systems. Structures of industries as well as social systems are to be reformed so that the sustainable relation between the human activities and natural environment can be established. The efforts of minimization of wastes as a first step will lead to the total utilization of resources or the increase of total productivity of the system. The material balance formula will be symbolically called "Zero Emissions" (figure 4.9). The possibilities of utilizing a waste from an industry as a raw material in itself or in another industry underlie the concept of a completely closed material balance and the total utilization of resources.

Material flow indicators

Two out of three indicators, namely resource productivity and cyclical use rate, decreased a little compared to FY2000 (table 4.6). Presumably the reduction of resource productivity derives from an increase in the input of natural resources by increased domestic excavation of stones and rock. The reduction of cyclical use rate can be traced to the increase of steel scrap export. Overall, the amount of final disposal was reduced compared to FY2000.

---

2 Including eco-designing, technologies for reuse, recycle and reduce, incineration technologies, technologies for final disposal, etc.

3 This approach involves returning to traditional furoshiki and mottainai values of consumption; enhancing education to improve the awareness of general public towards and developing green purchase activities.

4 A traditional Japanese phrase, meaning 'it is so wasteful that things are not made full use of their value"

Figure 4.7: Illustration of material flow in Japan for FY2000

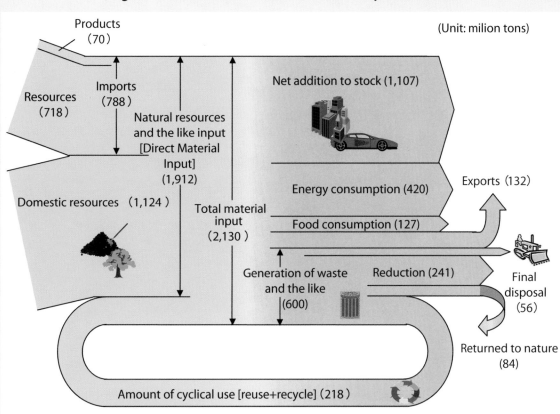

Table 4.5: Patterns and projection of material flow (FY2001-2010)

Indicators	FY2000	FY2001	FY2010
Resource productivity	281,000 yen/ton	275,000 yen/ton	390,000yen/ton
Cyclical use rate	10.2 per cent	9.9 per cent	14 per cent
Final disposal amount	57 million tons	53 million tons	28 million tons

Notes: Resource productivity =GDP/Input of natural resources and the like
Cyclical use rate= Amount of cyclical use (reuse and recycling)/input of natural resources and the like + amount of cyclical use
Source: Ministry of Environment, Japan

4.3.3 Japan's efforts to promoting the establishment of an International SMS

The amount of circulative resources generated is increasing at the global level due to international economic development and population growth, particularly in Asia. Meanwhile, the qualities of these resources are diversifying. International movement of circulative resources for recycling is also increasing. International flow of materials invokes concerns over environmental pollution and other problems related to these changes.

Issues related to the increasing amount of waste and transboundary movement of circulative resources are: (a) unqualified waste treatment businesses; (b) export of circulative resources and its impact on the domestic waste management and recycling system (hollowing out of Japan's domestic recycling industry), especially transboundary movement of hazardous waste (for the recipient countries).

More specific measures are based on a consensus that the international flow of goods and materials for recycling and remanufacturing can only take place when environment protection in importing countries is fully addressed. As the first step for planning international cooperation activities, capacity building programmes needs to be prioritized to enhance the national 3R capacity, taking into account developing countries' status quo. Meanwhile, for countries involved in the transboundary movement of recyclables, programmes and activities should be promoted to help build capacity for preventing environment pollution and reducing the barriers to the international flow.

Figure 4.8: Global material flow of plastics in 2004

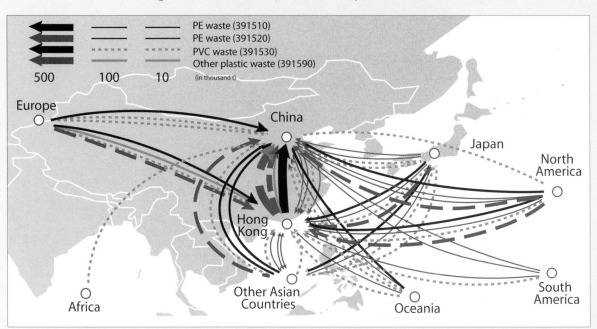

Source: Terazono, Atsushi (2006). Presentation made at the Asia 3R Conference held at Tokyo Japan October 30 – November 1, 2006

The proponents of 3R highlight the importance of the initiative inasmuch as its long and medium term outcomes ensure that:

- The 3Rs contribute to the economic development such as poverty eradication and more efficient production through creation of opportunities for benign cycle where environment and economic growth are mutually reinforcing;

- The 3Rs provide a firm basis for sustainable development through the improvement of water management which addresses environment problems such as soil and water contamination.

- Following up to the G8 development of the 3R Initiative and Action Plan, a Ministerial Conference on the 3R initiative was held in Japan in 2005, which triggered actual approaches in the respective countries based on the Initiative. The Senior Officials Meeting on the 3R Initiative was held in Japan in March 2006 for promoting further approaches through information exchange and other activities pertaining to recent progress.

In light of these changes, Japan is focusing their efforts to providing assistance for the promotion of zero-waste societies in developing countries, most notably in the forms of capacity building and technology cooperation especially in East Asia. Their strategies include:

- The establishment of SMS through national and local legislative and institutional leverages that share the spirit of *mottainai*. The formulation of visions and strategies that promote the 3Rs marks a major shift from unsustainable to sustainable consumption and production patterns. Regional and global efforts in information gathering and sharing, joint research and capacity building (strengthening legal frameworks, developing national strategies etc.) should be beneficial in promoting best practices of the 3Rs at local, national and international levels.

- Promoting the idea of facilitating import/export of circulative resources including the consideration of possibly removing trade barriers against the international flow of recycled and remanufactured goods and materials: definitely a very sensitive trade issue between developing and developed countries. However, in the context of 'maximization of resource efficiency and minimization of pollution' and if applied with proper mechanism, international flow of goods and materials for recycling and recycled products can be a desirable option for promoting sustainable consumption and production. This can be achieved by developing a list of environmental goods and services under the WTO Doha Mandate. Full compliance with the Basel Convention and Rotterdam Convention on Prior Informed Consent serves as a significant baseline. Moreover, criteria formulation and capacity building to distinguish waste from non-waste could pave the way for cross-border transfer of wastes or near-end-of-life products to developing countries. Complementary measures to dissipate concerns over transboundary waste transfer are international cooperation for improved monitoring for such material movements and the

Table 4.6: Linking the United Nations Millennium Development Goals with the 3Rs

Goals	3R Linkages
1. Eradicate extreme poverty	3R would promote systematic efforts and programmes on waste collection, waste recycling, and marketing of recyclable products, which would ultimately help generate employments, industrial activities, transportation, commerce, international trade and other benefits.
2. Achieve universal primary education	3R would promote systematic reduction and gradual abolishment of informal and unhealthy waste picking or collection practices, which has engage millions of children world wide depriving them to pursue their primary education.
3. Promote gender equality and empower women	Women disproportionately take care of many household activities such as cooking, childcare, shopping, domestic waste separation and disposal, etc. Appropriately advocated 3R awareness programmes would motivate their families to share their burden in waste sorting, separation and disposal in appropriate manner for achieving a recycled based society. The time saved could more productively used by women to take part in social and economic activities.
4. Reduce child mortality	Lack of access to clean land, clean water, and clean air is linked to child mortality in many developing countries. Systematic and efficient 3R programmes will ensure clean land, clean water and clean air – the fundamental rights of children and citizen.
5. Improve maternal health	Women are disproportionately affected by waste problems and living conditions with lack of access to clean land, clean water and clean air all of which contribute to poor maternal health conditions in both urban and rural areas of many developing countries. Systematic and efficient 3R programmes will ensure clean land, clean water and clean air – fundamental rights of every citizen.
6. Combat HIV/AIDs, malaria and other diseases	Effective and efficient waste management programmes coupled with systematic 3R programmes at local level will help healthy living environment in terms of clean water, air and land which are essential to combat disease like malaria and respiratory diseases.
7. Ensure environmental sustainability	Unsustainable production and consumption patterns coupled with insignificant recycle capability to replace virgin raw materials/natural resources, have contributed to many adverse impacts on environment (land, water, biodiversity, coastal and marine, atmosphere and climate, etc.) natural resources and human health. Effective and efficient 3R programmes are vital to reverse these trends of environmental unsustainability.
8. Develop a global partnership for development	Johannesburg Plan of Implementation (JPOI) in 2002 WSSD and subsequently, the 30th G8 Summit at Sea Island held at Georgia (8-10) June 2004) and the follow up 3R Ministerial Meeting at Tokyo (April 2005), have directly of indirectly emphasized the critical need for reorienting the production and consumption pattern through effective implementation of 3R (reduce, reuse and recycle) principles. These initiatives have recognized that the major cause of the continued deterioration of the global environment is the unsustainable pattern of consumption and production and have called upon countries to realize a globally sound material-cycle society through enhanced cooperation among various stakeholders (central governments, local governments, and through promotion of science and technology suitable for 3R and international trade of recyclables.

Source:<http://www.uncrd.or.jp/env/spc/docs/Table_1_MDG%20and%203R%20linkages-20Feb06.pdf> from UNCRD website.

development of a network in Asia that particularly prevents illegal trade of waste.

- Other areas of international cooperation may take place in spheres like: transfer of technologies through a regional centre approach; enhancing the linkage between the 3Rs to the United Nations Millennium Development Goals (MDGs) (table 4.6); connecting the 3Rs and climate change issues, with multilateral environmental agreements, Global Environmental Facility or Clean Development Mechanism being tools to promote the cooperation.

The various stakeholders from developing and developed countries involved in the 3R international cooperation undertake the following activities:

- private and public sector cooperation across states boost eco-friendly business with 3R principles, energy efficiency measures, cleaner production techniques, waste minimization techniques, and resource recovery and recycling techniques;

- central government authorities actively involved in promoting the institutionalization of 3R policies and legislations and providing an economic and political platform in line with the needs and demands of the local community;

Figure 4.9: Action plan to achieve the goal of 'zero-waste'

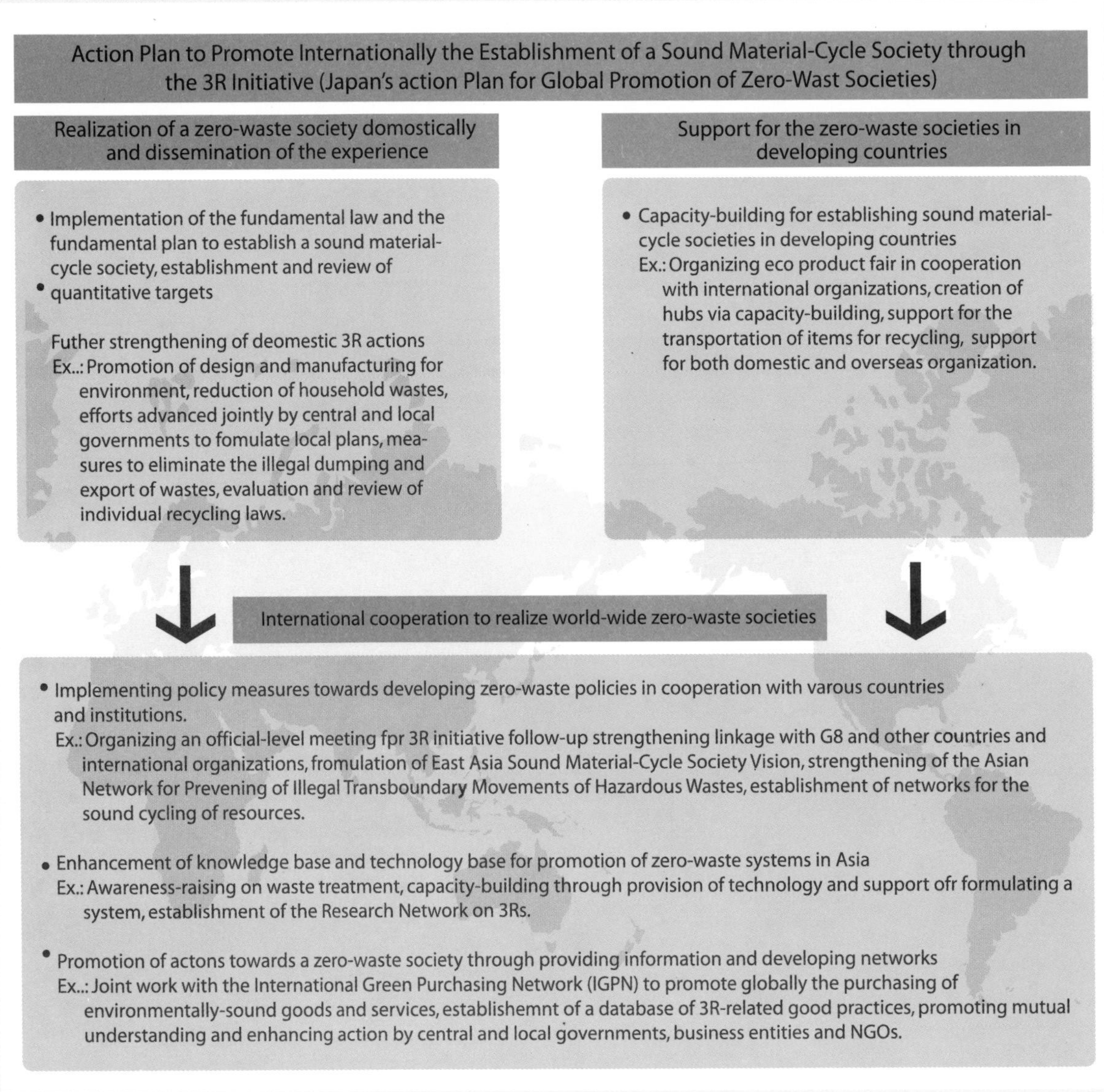

Action Plan to Promote Internationally the Establishment of a Sound Material-Cycle Society through the 3R Initiative (Japan's action Plan for Global Promotion of Zero-Wast Societies)	
Realization of a zero-waste society domostically and dissemination of the experience	**Support for the zero-waste societies in developing countries**
• Implementation of the fundamental law and the fundamental plan to establish a sound material-cycle society, establishment and review of • quantitative targets Futher strengthening of deomestic 3R actions Ex..: Promotion of design and manufacturing for environment, reduction of household wastes, efforts advanced jointly by central and local governments to fomulate local plans, measures to eliminate the illegal dumping and export of wastes, evaluation and review of individual recycling laws.	• Capacity-building for establishing sound material-cycle societies in developing countries Ex.: Organizing eco product fair in cooperation with international organizations, creation of hubs via capacity-building, support for the transportation of items for recycling, support for both domestic and overseas organization.

International cooperation to realize world-wide zero-waste societies

• Implementing policy measures towards developing zero-waste policies in cooperation with varous countries and institutions.
  Ex.: Organizing an official-level meeting fpr 3R initiative follow-up strengthening linkage with G8 and other countries and international organizations, fromulation of East Asia Sound Material-Cycle Society Vision, strengthening of the Asian Network for Prevening of Illegal Transboundary Movements of Hazardous Wastes, establishment of networks for the sound cycling of resources.

• Enhancement of knowledge base and technology base for promotion of zero-waste systems in Asia
  Ex.: Awareness-raising on waste treatment, capacity-building through provision of technology and support ofr formulating a system, establishment of the Research Network on 3Rs.

• Promotion of actons towards a zero-waste society through providing information and developing networks
  Ex..: Joint work with the International Green Purchasing Network (IGPN) to promote globally the purchasing of environmentally-sound goods and services, establishemnt of a database of 3R-related good practices, promoting mutual understanding and enhancing action by central and local governments, business entities and NGOs.

- provincial governments promote international cooperation for 3Rs, by collaborating with international partners to introduce to the public and implement 3R strategies and policies;

- donor communities (bilateral/multilateral donors) are encouraged to provide both financial and technical resources to promote international cooperation for 3Rs;

- scientific, research and academic institutions foster international collaborative research programmes to develop and transfer environmentally-sound technologies for 3Rs;

- NGOs and local community serve as an interface between local communities and international donors: acting on one hand as effective implementing agencies for 3R projects supported by international donors; and on the other hand, giving voice to local level stakeholders by spreading lessons of the best practices and sharing that with the international community who ultimately integrates the local needs and priorities in their projects and work programmes (figure 4.9).

In summing up, besides earnest efforts made at home, Japan is promoting SMS across Asia and the Pacific, North-East Asia in particular, with the view of raising the resource efficiency and sustainability and establishing a 'bio-region', where zero-waste is the primary and ultimate goal (figure 4.10).

5. FOLLOWING THROUGH THE ECO-EFFICIENCY AGENDA IN NORTH-EAST ASIA: THE NEXT ACTION STEPS

A small river, Cheonggyecheon, in a downtown of Seoul was covered with concrete in late 1960s.
The river came back to nature and people in 2003.

North-East Asia, as a region, is an ideal case for setting the standards for the development of national eco-efficiency policies. As a region with varying levels of development, and natural resource endowments, and an abundance of cultural traditions respective nature. North-East Asia can select and implement a wide variety of policy tools to affect different sectors of the economy and society. As already exhibited in Chapter 4, North-East Asian countries are moving forward in sustainable development through various policy initiatives. This foundation is promising and should continue to be strengthened, especially though a focus on resource productivity and dematerialization. Efforts in North-East Asia should focus on strengthening existing regional environmental cooperation, expanding current eco-efficiency efforts to reach more sectors of society, and prioritizing changes in the local, national, and regional economic growth patterns.

Eco-efficiency in North-East Asia needs to proceed on a three part policy path: micro-level, macro-level, and meta-level. Each national government in North-East Asia needs to develop eco-efficiency policies unique to their situation that will allow them to maximize eco-efficiency for the most appropriate sectors, such as energy, transportation, infrastructure, and residential sectors. Additionally, policies should be directed at different target groups, such as business, civil society, governments, and subregions. A coordinated, regional level approach for macro-level eco-efficiency will guide North-East Asia towards a new and sustainable pattern of economic growth.

5.1 Harnessing eco-efficiency in North-East Asia

Practical ways to harness eco-efficiency at the macro-level include engaging a number of policy tools to address production and consumption, the private sector, civil society, and individuals. There are a wide range of options, but can be divided into a few sections, namely market-based instruments, regulatory instruments, voluntary measures, and information-based measures (Ekins and Tomei, 2006). Until recently, many governments have focused on regulatory instruments, such as command-and-control legislation that prohibits the use of certain technologies or mandates the use of others. Many more governments are beginning to shift towards a mixed slate of policy choices, with a number of market-based incentives. The key to harnessing eco-efficiency is to use a wide range of policy tools to affect a large scope of society and inspire behavioral changes.

The WBCSD offers twelve key action points for an eco-efficient future, which seek to present a holistic approach for achieving economy-wide eco-efficiency (WBCSD, 2000).

Government leaders and civil servants:

- Set macro-economic efficiency targets and conversion criteria for sustainable development;

- Integrate policy measures to strengthen eco-efficiency (e.g. eliminate subsidies, internalize externalities, and effect shifts environmentally harmful in tax policy);

- Work toward changing international policy rules and systems for trade, financial transactions, etc, to support higher resource productivity and emissions reduction, as well as improvements for the underprivileged.

Civil society leaders and consumers:

- Encourage consumers to prefer eco-efficient, more sustainable products and services;

- Support political measures to create the framework conditions which reward eco-efficiency.

Educators:

- Include eco-efficiency and sustainability in high school and university curricula and build it into research and development programmes.

Financial analysts and investors:

- Recognize and reward eco-efficiency and sustainability as investment criteria;

- Help eco-efficient companies and sustainability leaders to communicate their progress and related business benefits to financial markets;

- Promote and use assessment tools and sustainability ratings to support the markets and to help widen understanding of eco-efficiency's benefits.

Business leaders:

- Integrate eco-efficiency into business strategies, including operational, product innovation and marketing strategies;

- Report company eco-efficiency and sustainability performance openly to stakeholders;

- Support policy measures which reward eco-efficiency.

The WBCSD, in combination with the above key points, stresses the importance of establishing indicators and targets for measuring eco-efficiency, and believe that governments can establish national eco-efficiency strategies founded upon such targets

and indicators. The OECD, as mentioned earlier, supports the idea of decoupling, and this can be a starting point for governments wishing to set targets. For example, by striving to achieve both absolute and relative decoupling of economic growth from environmental pressures, governments will be able to not only improve environmental conditions but will enhance quality of life standards.

Germany has already begun to implement economy-wide eco-efficiency measures with their Green Tax Reform. Tax and budget reforms are among the most powerful policy tools that can help drive an eco-efficient society. In 1999, Germany introduced the "Ökosteuer" (eco-tax) as a way to address the rising energy demand, greenhouse gas emissions, high labour costs, and losses in competitiveness. Because labour costs are already exceptionally high in Germany, it was important to help find ways for German businesses to cut costs while stimulating innovation. The eco-tax addressed both of these issues. By placing a tax on fuel, Germany aimed to reduce fuel consumption (thereby emissions). At the same time, this provided incentives for German firms to be more innovative in their production methods. The tax revenue is used to contribute to the pension funds so that employers can also contribute less in terms of labour costs. Since 1999 the eco-tax has been reformed twice in order to address some of the weaknesses and enhance the positive environmental outcomes of the tax.

Green GDP has been widely discussed as a way to help national economies become more environmentally sustainable. It also promotes the valuation of ecosystem services and raises awareness of the dependency of sustainability on natural resources. There are a number of ways that Green GDP is being applied. Green tax reform, as already highlighted in the case of Germany, is becoming one of the more popular ways to encourage and harness eco-efficiency. By taxing pollution or inefficiency use of resources, rather than income, governments can reward eco-efficiency while delinking economic activity from environmental degradation. Additionally, some countries have tried to alter the perception of economic wealth by introducing concepts such as the Sufficiency Economy in Thailand of Gross Domestic Happiness in Bhutan. These two approaches consider happiness and well-being to be dependent not just on the economic production of an economy, but the environmental and social conditions as well. By promoting sufficiency, Thailand is trying to shift consumption patterns to be more eco-efficient and focused on real needs and happiness rather than material accumulation.

Green Growth, a concept being widely promoted in the Asia Pacific region and, as already mentioned, was adopted by the 2005 MCED as a practical path for sustainable development in the region. Green growth begins by building eco-efficient societies that consume more efficiently and increase the efficiency of resource use in production processes. It looks at economies as a whole, the interactions among sectors, and aims to reduce the social vulnerability of a society while investing in natural capital in order to maintain or enhance biocapacity for long-term sustainability.

5.2 Next steps for North-East Asia

As already discussed in this paper, moving towards eco-efficient consumption is probably the most important, yet most difficult, task ahead for North-East Asia. By first undertaking a study at the current status of eco-efficiency in the various national economies in the region, North-East Asia will be able to determine the necessary next steps for moving towards an eco-efficient society. Already many countries in North-East Asia are undertaking efforts to improve eco-efficiency. Notwithstanding the on-going efforts, the following suggests some next steps for promoting eco-efficiency in North-East Asia.

5.2.1 Government actions

At the macro-, economy-wide level, North-East Asian countries should build and support a societal consensus on the objective of sustainable development in an eco-efficiency framework. Governments need to reform their public policies in order to promote eco-efficient production and consumption at all levels, including government activities, consumer and producer activities, and international policies and regulations. Currently many governments have in place policies that actively discourage resource efficiency. For example, fuel subsidies for industry allow firms to ignore the true costs of energy for production, thereby resulting in wasteful use with little incentive to change their behavior. If North-East Asia recognizes the importance of reduced fuel consumption and efficient use of energy resources, then governments should create incentives for industry to alter production patterns to enable energy efficiency.

The first step for government action in regards to eco-efficiency is identifying policies that discourage eco-inefficiency and introduce incentives for eco-efficiency. This will build a solid foundation for further macro-level policies to promote sustainable development through eco-efficiency. Following the identification of perverse incentives for inefficiency, national governments should adopt economy-wide reforms in the form of adopting Green GDP or Green Tax initiatives. They can additionally implement measures to utilize full cost accounting across all levels and sectors of society. Full cost accounting takes into account all costs associated with a given activity, including social, environmental, and long-term costs. The integration of environmental accounting into government activities will build a culture of accountability for actions and impacts on the environment and thereby greater social welfare.

Additionally, national governments are in a unique position to make a dramatic effect on consumer behavior. This can be achieved through similar measures as mentioned above, e.g. eco-taxes, incentives for reducing consumption of energy and water or utilizing public transportation. For example, in the water sector, governments can use varied water pricing structures such as volumetric-measured, increasing-block tariffs, which means that users are charged for the amount of water they use, and that as the use increases, the per unit charge also increases. This would help reduce household consumption of water, but would have a much greater impact on industrial and agricultural consumption of water, which accounts for about 85 per cent of worldwide use of water supplies. National governments can also provide incentives for technological innovation in regards to the use of water in production processes. It is essential that North-East Asia adjust the patterns of water consumption towards eco-efficiency because of the relative scarcity of water resources in the region.

The government can also make great strides in altering consumer behavior in the energy sector. Energy efficiency can be addressed through pricing mechanisms, similar to the water pricing scheme suggested above , and raising, public awareness about the true costs of energy consumption and ways to reduce household consumption. To address energy consumption by industry, policy options include providing rewards for targeted reductions in use as well as providing incentives for technological innovation.

The transportation sector offers numerous opportunities to alter consumer behavior over the long-term. For example, rather than planning new highways to prepare for projected future growth in personal automobile use, governments can invest the money in railway infrastructure and in incentives for consumers to use public transportation instead of personal vehicles. By planning for future increases in the need for transportation infrastructure and choosing more sustainable options, governments can alter the mindsets of citizens gradually over time.

Governments should utilize their influence at the international level to help change international policy rules, regulations, and systems for trade

Box 5.1: Case study: Basque Country

In 2003, Basque Country in Spain issued a report measuring the eco-efficiency of its economy in relation to the European Union. It is one of the first attempts to measure the eco-efficiency of a region; the Basque Country evaluated eco-efficiency based on a set of eco-efficiency indicators that "reflect the extent of decrease in the use of resources and energy and the reduction in pressure on the environment associated with products and services marketed." The general indicators used by the Basque Country include the municipal solid waste produced per capita (MSW), final energy consumption, greenhouse gas emissions (GHG), emissions of acidifiers, total material requirement per capita (TMR), GDP, and the unemployment rate. Sector specific indicators were also used: industrial output index (IOI) and hazardous waste production for the industry sector; tons per kilometre, kilometres of motorway and dual carriageway, and emissions of tropospheric ozone precursors (TOPS) for the transportation sector; gross added value (GAV) and TOPs emissions for the energy sector; and the number of cars and private spending for the residential sector. Through the measurement and application of these indicators to its economy, the Basque Country was able to determine the following results with an eye towards improved policies promoting eco-efficiency:

- Overall eco-efficiency for Basque Country decreased from 1990 to 2000, despite the relative delinking of economic growth from the environment;

- In the industry sector, pressure on the environment decreased while economic activity in the sector increased;

- Eco-efficiency in the transportation sector has decreased mainly due to significant growth in the sector coupled with rebound effects;

- The energy sector had mixed results with increased in GHG emissions coinciding with increased economic activity, while the emissions of acidifiers decreased (although this decrease is attributed to the decrease in coke manufacturing);

- Consumption has greatly increased and is accompanied by increased pressures on the environment, meaning decreased eco-efficiency.

Increases in eco-efficiency of the Basque Country are driven by regulation, technology, and structural factors, particularly in the industrial sector.

In its 2003 report, the Basque Country recognized some key areas for consideration as it moves forward with eco-efficiency policies:

1) In regards to industry, the Basque Country recognized that, because the industrial sector is subject to monitoring and regulation by the government, the levels of pollution have generally gone done. The task at hand is to evaluate to what extent the governments policies have been effective in reducing the pressure on the environment by industry.

2) In the transportation sector, the Basque Country identified a need to delink economic growth from the "need for mobility," meaning that expanding economic activity needs to find more efficiency ways of dispersing its outcomes throughout society.

3) The importance of the energy sector was highlighted in its contributions to overall economic activity as well as its own direct pressures on the environment. By delinking the economic growth from environmental pressures, the Basque Country will be able to achieve significant improvements in overall environmental quality.

4) Consumption was identified as one of the greatest challenges, because environmental pressures "associated with consumer habits are more difficult to deal with" than those arising from industry, transportation, or the energy sector.

These considerations highlight challenges that are applicable to almost any economy, particularly with regards to consumer behavior. North-East Asia, when developing ways to harness eco-efficiency in the region and in individual countries, can use cases like the Basque Country to help formulate policies.

Source: Basque Country Government. Eco-efficiency 2003. Environmental Framework Programme Series, 21 May 2003

and financial transactions. These actions include altering the perception that incentives for decreasing environmental degradation are barriers to trade. Additionally, by supporting and advocating for higher resource productivity and emissions reductions, the governments of North-East Asia will help shift the region towards a more eco-efficient mindset for future economic growth patterns.

5.2.2 Business sector actions

Private corporations and firms have been the starting point for eco-efficiency for more countries in the world. It is clear that, without the participation of the private sector, society will not be able to achieve its eco-efficiency goals. To that end, the private sector has a special role to play in shaping certain patterns of economic growth and can help lead nations towards eco-efficient consumption and production. It is important to bear in mind that the private sector alone cannot achieve eco-efficiency for society and governments need to support actions of the business sector through a reward or merit system that recognizes the positive eco-efficiency impacts. Businesses should:

- Integrate eco-efficiency into their business strategy, including their operational, product innovation and marketing strategies. This means the permeation of eco-efficiency at all levels of operation in a business. As demonstrated by Toyota, it is possible to affect an entire supply chain and ensure eco-efficiency of a line of products on a larger scale.

- Report corporate eco-efficiency and sustainability performance openly to stakeholders. Corporations are realizing the value that is associated by consumers with corporate responsibility, which includes the eco-efficiency of company's operations and products. Reporting their efforts provides more concrete value to a business' efforts and also contributes to the awareness of consumers and helps them to make better choices about where and how they spend their money.

- Support policy measures which reward eco-efficiency. The private sector can play a very powerful role in a society, given its role as a driver for economic growth. Business should use this power to promote eco-efficiency across society, which will benefit not only itself, but all of society, for generations to come.

5.2.3 Civil society actions

Civil society is extremely important for promoting eco-efficiency, especially with regards to their potential impact on the eco-efficiency of consumption. While government actions can clearly

and rapidly alter the eco-efficiency of production by working with businesses, civil society can provide a framework and a message for consumption, the long-neglected side of eco-efficiency patterns of economic activities. Civil society should:

- Promote a major psychological and cultural shift from 'having towards being'. In some countries, such as Thailand, this is dubbed as a "sufficiency economy" – happiness does not come from the things that we have and consume, but from being part of a family and community and contributing towards the growth and opportunities therein. By promoting a shift in mindset, civil society will greatly contribute to the success of achieving economy-wide eco-efficiency.

- Encourage consumers to prefer eco-efficient and sustainable products and services. This involves public education and outreach on what types of services and products are eco-efficient, as well as tips on being an aware and responsible consumer.

- Support political measures to create the framework conditions which reward eco-efficiency. Civil society can, through political support, advocate for overall change in a nation's economic patterns of growth, addressing both the production and consumption sides of eco-efficiency.

5.2.4 Regional actions

Regional efforts towards eco-efficiency should build a common vision for an eco-efficient society. NEASPEC, as an intergovernmental mechanism, can help establish this common vision and raise awareness by working with member countries in facilitating discussions for improving resource efficiency and disseminating information on eco-efficient practices across various sectors. It can start by undertaking comparative assessment of how countries in the North-East Asian region are faring in their efforts to attain eco-efficiency, distilling lessons from both the successes and failure of the efforts for which countries can learn and base their future eco-efficiency strategies.

Similarly NEASPEC can also stimulate the promotion of eco-efficiency initiatives through capacity development, such as training programmes about eco-efficient practices across sectors and levels of society that will help strengthen the national, as well as regional, an efforts for achieving eco-efficient societies. Additionally, NEASPEC can support and encourage information sharing and policy consultations, thereby assisting countries in institutionalizing policy frameworks for eco-efficiency.

Steps in this direction have already been taken following the decision of the Twelfth Senior Officials

Meeting in March 2007 to launch the Eco-Efficiency Partnership in North-East Asia. On this basis, NEASPEC will now develop a platform for joint activities for the promotion of eco-efficiency in the subregion. By employing multilateral actions mentioned above, NEASPEC will contribute to a sound foundation for an eco-efficient future for NEASPEC countries.

5.3 Concluding remarks

The path to sustainable development is never easy, often daunting, as society are impelled to make difficult choices that are dictated by the values and interests of stakeholders acting individually or collectively. The paradigm challenges most of the conventional wisdom founded from generations of experience and by which society have grown to live with. The aspect of sustainable development, which many find daunting to undertake, is changing the current patterns of consumption and production. Many models have been looked at and as repeatedly mentioned in the previous chapters, no single formula can fully address the complex social, economic and environmental issues societies face. The compulsion for change and the choices of the probable outcomes are central to the model. Among the numerous sustainable development models that have been examined, eco-efficiency with all its positive attributes and limitations offers the most pragmatic approach to attaining the goals of environmental sustainability. In its totality, eco-efficiency demands change and provides opportunities for society to discern which choices can lead to at least *"simultaneously satisfying the rising consumption of an expanding population and attaining a reasonable environmental quality"* (Huppes and Ishikawa, 2005). This publication covered discussions on an alternative to the current path of development: a choice by which governments, private sector and civil society as whole can make and collectively take actions. Overall the pursuit of real sustainable development demands societies to take both a revolutionary and an evolutionary path: revolutionary because it compels societies to radically think and critically question the conventional understanding of development, a pattern that definitely will not lead to sustainability; evolutionary, and citing Meadows, because it arises from the vision, insights, experiments and actions of billions of people, requiring every human quality and skill, from technical ingenuity, economic entrepreneurship, and political leadership to the very intrinsic human values of honesty, compassion and understanding (Meadows, 1992).

REFERENCES

AQUASTAT accessed online on 12 July 2006 at <www.fao.org/ag/agl/aglw/aquastat/main/index.stm FAO AQUASTAT online database.>.

Alex Kirby: BBC Online 'North Korea's Environment Crisis', accessed online on 2 August 2006 at <http://news.bbc.co.uk/2/hi/science/nature/3598966.stm>

Bank of Korea (BOK), "Future of the Asian Economy," 2005.

BASF <http://corporate.basf.com/en/sustainability/oekonomie/produktion.htm?id=XxIZM9*WDbcp1SX Accessed 25 July 2005>

Cramer Jacqueline, Responsiveness of Industry to eco-efficiency improvements in the product chain: the case of Akzo Nobel. Paper presented at the Greening of Industry Conference Rome November 15-18 1998 accessed on 15 January 2007 at <www.p2pays.org/ref/26/25555.pdf>

Department of Economic and Social Affairs (DESA) (2006). The Millennium Development Indicators accessed on 12 December 2006 at <http://mdgs.un.org/unsd/mdg/default.aspx>.

(2002) Johannesburg Plan of Implementation accessed on 1 December 2006 at <www.un.org/esa/sustdev/documents/WSSD_POI_PD/English/POIToc.htm>.

Desimone, Livio and Frank Popoff (1997). "Eco-efficiency: The business link to sustainable development". Cambridge, Massachusetts, MIT Press

Downs, Erica (2006) Energy Security Series: China, The Brookings Foreign Policy Studies accessed at </www.brookings.edu/fp/research/energy/2006china.htm > on 15 March 2007

Ekins, Paul and Julia Tomei (2006). "Eco-efficiency of Consumption and Production Patterns in Asia and the Pacific." ESCAP Study. Bangkok, Thailand.

Ekins, Paul (2006). "Eco-efficiency and Resource Productivity: Concepts, Indicators and Trends in Asia-Pacific" Presentation. 23-25 May 2006, Beijing, China.

ESCAP (2006). State of the Environment in Asia and the Pacific 2005. Bangkok, Thailand

ESCAP (2005). Review of Developments in Transport in Asia and the Pacific 2005, New York

Esty, Daniel C., MarcA. Levy, tanja Srebotnjak, Alexander de Sherbinin, Christian H. Kim and Brifget Anderson (2006). Pilot 2006 Environmental Performance Index. New haven: Yale Center for Environmental Law and Policy

Gross, Robert and Tim Foxon (2003), Policy support for innovation to secure improvements in resource productivity, International Journal Environment and Technology, vol.3, No$_2$, 2003 p118-130 accessed at <www.hm-treasury.gov.uk/media/F72/F3/Gross_Foxon_03.pdf>
on 2 February 2007.

Grossman, Gene M., and Alan B. Krueger (1991). "Environmental Impacts of a North American Free Trade Agreement", National Bureau of Economic Research Working Paper no. 3914.

Grossman, Gene M., and Alan B. Krueger (1995). "Pollution and Technology: what do we know? In I. Goldin and L.A. Winters (Eds) The Economics of Sustainable Development, Cambridge University Press, Cambridge.

Hawken, Paul (1993). The Ecology of Commerce. HarperCollins New York

Hanson, Arthur and Martin Claude (2006). "One Lifeboat: China and the World's Environment and Development, International Institute for Sustainable Development, Canada.

Hertwich, Edgar G. (2005)."Consumption and the Rebound Effect." Journal of Industrial Ecology, 9:1-2. p. 86.

Department of Economic and Social Affairs (DESA). The Millennium Development Indicators accessed on 12 December 2006 at <http://mdgs.un.org/unsd/mdg/default.aspx>.

Energy Information Agency (EIA) accessed on 10 August 2006 at <www.eia.doe.gov/environment.html>.

Huppes, Gjult and Masanobu Ishikawa (2005). " A Framework for Quantified Eco-Efficiency Analysis" published in the Journal of Industrial Ecology (Vo. 9 no. 4) MIT Press, Cambridge Massachusetts

IEA (2006). Energy balances of OECD countries 2003-2004; and Energy balances of non-OECD countries 2003-2004 (Paris, OECD/IEA)

IEA (2004). World Energy Outlook, Paris, OECD/IEA

IEA (2005). Key World Energy Statistics 2005, Paris, OECD/IEA.

Jalas, Mikko, Andrius Plepys, and Maria Elander (2001). "Workshop 10 – Sustainable Consumption and Rebound Effect." Workshop of the 7th ERCP, Lund, Sweden. May 2001.

McDonough, W. and Michael Braungart (1998). the Next Industrial Revolution, The Atlantic Monthly ,Volume 282, No. 4; pages 82-92. October 1998

Meadows, Donella H., Dennis L. Meadows and Jorgen Randers (1992). Beyond the Limits, Chealsea Green Publishing, Vermont

National Conference of State Legislatures (1996). "Glossary of Electric Utility Restructuring Terms" accessed on 12 January 2007 at <www.ncsl.org/programs/energy/glossary.htm>

OECD (2002). "Indicators to Measure Decoupling of Environmental Pressure from Economic Growth." SG/SD (2002) 1 / FINAL. 16 May 2002.

Schmidt-Bleek, Friedrich (1999). "Factor 10/MIPS Concept: Bridging Ecological, Economic, and Social Dimensions with Sustainability Indicators." Zero emissions Forum, United Nations University, Tokyo Japan.

State Environmental Planning Agency (2006), "China Green National Accounting Study Report 2004" accessed on 17 March 2007 at <http://english.sepa.gov.cn/zwxx/xwfb/200609/t20060908_92580.htm >.

See "Improving Energy Efficiency in Asia: a policy review." UNEP. 2006.

Strachan, Janet R., Georgina Ayre, Jan McHarry, and Rosalie Callway (2005). "The Plain Language Guide to the World Summit on Sustainable Development", London: Earthscan, 2005.

Toshiba (2006) Social and Environmental Activities accessed on 26 July 2006 at

<http://www.toshiba.co.jp/env/en/management/factor_t.htm>.

Toyota Environmental and Social Report 2005, accessed on 25 July 2005 at <http://corporate.basf.com/en/sustainability/grundwerte/leitlinien.htm?id=XxIZM9*WDbcp1SX>.

UNCED (1992). "Agenda 21: Programme of Action for Sustainable Development" United Nations, New York.

UNCTAD (2004). "A Manual for the Preparers and Users of Eco-efficiency Indicators." Version 1.1, New York.

UNEP(2001) "Energy Efficiency: promotion of energy efficiency in industry and financing of investments." United Nations: New York

Von Weizsäcker, Ernst, Amory Lovins and L. Hunter Lovins (1997) . Factor Four: doubling wealth and halving resource use. London: Earthscan.

WBCSD (1999), "Eco-efficiency Indicators: A Tool for Better Decision-Making.".

WBCSD (2000). "Eco-efficiency: creating more value with less impact." August . p.29

World Bank (2004). "World Development Indicators 2004", Washington DC World Bank.

World Watch Institute. "Vital Signs 2005." W.W. Norton Publishing New York.

World Wide Fund for Nature (WWF) (1998). "Living Planet Report 1998" , Gland, Switzerland.

WWF (2006). "Living Planet Report 2006" Gland, Switzerland.

WWF (2005). "Asia-Pacific 2005: The Ecological Footprint," accessed online July 06, 2006 at <http://assets.panda.org/downloads/asialpr2005.pdf> p.3-12

Wuppertal Institute. Accessed online 18 July 2006._<http://www.wupperinst.org/FactorFour/FactorFour_FAQ.html>